DE PROPRIETATIBUS LITTERARUM

edenda curat

C. H. VAN SCHOONEVELD

Indiana University

Series Practica, 99

S-14-P-2-
JJ

COMIC CHARACTER IN RESTORATION DRAMA

by

AGNES V. PERSSON

1975

MOUTON

THE HAGUE · PARIS

ISBN 90 279 3321 9

Printed in The Netherlands

TABLE OF CONTENTS

I

AN UNEXAMINED LIFE

(A Theory of Comic Character)

> To view the infirmities of human nature in perspective
> is the special province of comedy.[1]

Plato not only is a master in creating comic characters who are unaware of their own limitations, but also he often defines their natures. He describes those who live an unexamined life as ignorant people who do not "seek the truth or crave to be made wise. And, indeed, what makes their case so hopeless is that, having neither beauty, nor goodness, nor intelligence, they are statisfied with what they are, and do not long for the virtues they have never missed."[2] Plato reiterates this idea in the *Philebus,* when after stating that the ridiculous arises from lack of self-knowledge, he points out three ways in which ignorance of self can be shown in man: "First, in respect of wealth, he may think himself richer than his property makes him. ... But there are even more who think themselves taller and more handsome and physically finer in general than they really and truly are. ... But far the greatest number are mistaken as regards the third class of things, namely possessions of the soul. They think themselves superior in virtue, when they are not."[3] Plato deplores lack of self-knowledge and labels those furthest from following the Delphic inscription "Know Thyself" as comic characters.

Plato is not the only one who believes that some kind of ignorance is an essential trait of a comic character. In the sixteenth century, Vincenzo Maggi, in his treatise *On the Ridiculous*, attempts to classify the causes of laughter, and in doing so, he looks for the source of the ridiculous. He examines first the classical theories of comic character, but finds them somewhat limited. Although he accepts Aristotle's and Cice-

---

[1] Cyrus E. Hoy, *The Hyacinth Room* (New York: Knopf, 1964), p. 36.
[2] Plato, *The Collected Dialogues*, "Symposium", ed. Edith Hamilton and Huntington Cairns (Pantheon, 1966; first printing, 1961), p. 556.
[3] Plato, *The Collected Dialogues*, "Philebus", p. 1130.

ro's tenets that the source of laughter is physical ugliness, baseness and deformity, he does realize that these traits do not satisfactorily explain all that is ridiculous in a human being. Maggi is aware that not only the deformity of the body but also deformity of the soul and mind can be comic. He turns to Plato's writings for support and states that in "the *Sophist* Plato says that this baseness is a great and varied ignorance. And rightly so. For the knowledge of our mind is so natural that the mind seems to have been given as a gift from a very great and good God to man for the sake of knowledge; now in general to withdraw from what is natural to itself is to slip into baseness; certainly, then, ignorance, since it is nothing else than a withdrawal of knowledge, will be the baseness of the mind."[4] Ignorance, according to Maggi, is the deformity of the soul, it is the baseness of the mind, and a "lack of knowledge about those things which are commonly known by others, and which are evident from their own nature".[5]

Lodovico Castelvetro, another sixteenth century Italian critic, states that "the proper objects for comedy to imitate are stupid and ugly persons who are neither harmed nor pained by their stupidity or ugliness".[6] The word "stupid" is Castelvetro's addition to the orginal theory. He does not look back to Greek and Latin comedy for examples but examines Boccaccio's characters with the classical theories in mind. Since many of the great comic characters in *The Decameron* are neither ugly nor deformed, the Italian scholar soon forgets about the statements made in the *Poetics* and writes about those who are "wanting in common sense, and who are simple-minded and stupid". Physical shortcomings become less important than mental deficiences and the ridiculous personages are those who are "ignorant of the world and its ways".[7]

Castelvetro recognizes that a comic character is usually the victim of some kind of deception. He lists four kinds of deceptions. First, "Some men are deceived through their ignorance of things that are commonly known among men, and through drunkenness, dreams, and delirium." Here he echoes Maggi's thoughts on the same subject. Castelvetro offers as an example Calandrino from *The Decameron*, "who believes in the miraculous reports of the country of Bengodi, and who

---

[4] Vincenzo Maggi, "On the Ridiculous", in Paul Lauter, *Theories of Comedy*, ed. and intro. Paul Lauter (New York, 1964), p. 67.
[5] *Ibid.*
[6] Lodovico Castelvetro, "Commentary on Artistotle's 'Poetics' ", in Lauter, p. 88.
[7] Castelvetro, in Lauter, p. 90.

also believes that he is with child, that a woman who is touched with a talisman must follow him, and that he has found the heliotrope, a stone of miraculous powers".[8]

Then Castelvetro mentions those who are deceived "through their ignorance of the arts and sciences, or of the true measure of their own physical and intellectual powers, as when one who has an exaggerated notion of his powers boasts that he is able to do what in reality he cannot do".[9] This observation reminds one of Plato's statements made in the *Philebus*; Castelvetro, however, combines lack of self-knowledge with a boastful nature when he describes the victims of the second kind of deception. He states that ignorance of arts and sciences is not "ridiculous in itself, nor is the ignorance of some fact or the inability to do some particular thing; what is ridiculous is the pretense to greater intellectual and physical powers than one actually possesses and the failure of the powers when they are put to the test, with the consequent discovery by the boaster that he has been the victim of self-deception".[10]

The last two deceptions mentioned by Castelvetro are not due to the inadequacy of character and lack of self-knowledge but to other causes: "Some are deceived when a thing or a saying is given an unexpected turn or when their own words are turned against them", and "Some are deceived through the machinations of others and chances."[11]

Since Plato, Maggi, and Castelvetro, many, from the Renaissance to our time, have observed that lack of knowledge can be comic. Those who are concerned with the theory of comedy, those who create great comic characters and those who analyze these creations discover that unawareness in all its kaleidoscopic variations is the subject of comic literature. Unawareness and ignorance are not necessarily comic, but a comic character is usually ignorant in some way.

One can clearly distinguish between two kinds of ignorance: first, lack of awareness induced by external circumstances, and second, lack of awareness due to the inherent nature of the character. The first one is short-lived and can affect all men because even the most circumspect are occasionally unaware of their situation. "Who cannot be crushed with a plot", says Parolles in *All's Well that Ends Well*. In this category

[8] *Ibid.*
[9] Castelvetro, pp. 89-90.
[10] Castelvetro, p. 91.
[11] Castelvetro, p. 90.

we find Castelvetro's fourth group, those who are deceived through the machinations of others or of chance. There are many devices by which the cleverest can be made blind to facts; disguise, secret conspiracy, lies, comic misunderstandings, exchange of identities, etc. In all these instances we deal with irony of situation. Since most possibilities of this kind of unawareness have been analyzed and explained by Bertrand Evans in his book, *Shakespeare's Comedies,* I shall discuss the second group, those whose unawareness is often permanent and is an innate quality of their character. Here we deal with irony of character. The reader is aware of the shortcomings and deficiencies in the character, but the comic character, who lives an unexamined life, is unable to perceive them.

Ignorance is manifold and varied. A person has to acquire many fields of knowledge, in life or on the stage, to be considered a fairly civilized and not too ridiculous human being. If he fails to do so and there is a considerable gap of awareness in his knowledge then he can expect correction and ridicule. Thus, first of all, different areas of knowledge will be examinel in the attempt to define the nature of comic character. Second, the degree of knowledge, or rather ignorance, will be explored, and, finally, some remarks will be made about the nature of the comic character and the attitude of the reader toward him.

The special knowledge which is required from a character depends on the criteria established by the writer in his work. In one case it is the proper way of speaking and behaving, in another, the knowledge of the right values. If the character is unable or unwilling to meet the demands made upon him he is judged by his fellow characters and the audience, and is punished with laughter.

"The comic character is judged according the manner of his peers, or the science of psychology, or the laws of morality", says Potts in his treatise on comedy.[12] One can perhaps add to this that a comic character is also judged according to the standards of intelligence established in the literary work. In the rustic world of Calandrino the requirements are fewer and the standards lower than in the urbane realm of Restoration and Edwardian comedy. Sometimes common sense is the sign of the right kind of intelligence as is often the case in Molière's comedies. In addition to a certain degree of intelligence, a character must usually be aware of human beings, of his own nature and the nature of others. The knowledge of values, morals, and professional ethics is often the

---

[12]   L. J. Potts, *Comedy* (New York, 1966), p. 115.

main requirement in the didactic comedies of Jonson, whereas in Restoration comedies the emphasis is on awareness of the ways of the fashionable world. Thus the fields of knowledge discussed in the following pages will be the general intelligence of characters in comedy, their knowledge of human beings, of values, and of manners.

The author has many ways by which he can convey the measure of intelligence. The education of a person sometimes indicates his mental standards. Congreve's Mirabell is well acquainted with Waller and Suckling, Molière's Cléante quotes Montaigne, and Shaw's Cusins recites long passages from Euripides' *Bacchae*. On the other hand, the Petkoff's library in Shaw's comic Bulgaria contains only "a single fixed shelf stocked with old paper-covered novels, broken-backed, coffee-stained, torn and thumbed; and a couple of little hanging shelves with a few gift books on them". The library is a visible manifestation of the Petkoff family's lack of erudition and sophistication.

At times the author takes advantage of the rather simple device of "dressing up" a character in his mental qualities. Bottom wears an ass's head and Malvolio's lack of perception is conveyed by his manner of dress. The fop's vanity is betrayed by the mode of his attire and the cuckold's horns show that he has been victimized, thanks to his gullibility or folly.

A person often reveals his shortcomings by the way he speaks and thinks. The French are masters in depicting comic characters who are unable to reason logically. In Voltaire's *Candide* Pangloss explains, "our noses were made to carry spectacles, so we have spectacles. Legs were clearly intended for breeches, and we wear them. ... And since pigs were made to be eaten, we eat pork all year round." Candide's unawareness is conveyed by his use of faulty syllogisms, *non sequiturs*; and, Martin tries to convince his friend that men are evil and vicious by false analogy. When a man like Pangloss lets his life be ruled by an illogical theory, he inevitably becomes ridiculous. In Molière's *School for Wives*, Arnolphe, who wishes to wed a young girl and avoid being cuckolded, creates his own, foolproof theory about the nature of a successful marriage. He believes that knowledge corrupts and only those who are ignorant are good people. Consequently, he keeps Agnes, his future bride, uneducated and shut away from the world and staffs his house with simple-minded fools. Arnolphe has to pay dearly for his fallacious theory and his unintelligent way of thinking.

While the French excel in depicting those who lack logic, the English writers are masters of creating comic characters who do not know how to use words properly. Dogberry's ignorance and Slip-Slop's untidy mind are revealed the moment they begin to speak. The classical example is Mrs. Malaprop who asks her niece to "illiterate" her suitor from her memory and "extirpate" herself from the relationship. In her discussion with Sir Anthony, she proposes a new school curriculum for young girls; she would eliminate "Greek, or Hebrew, or Algebra, or Simony, or Fluxions, or Paradoxes", but she would have her niece "instructed in geometry, that she might know something of the contagious countries – but above all, Sir Anthony, she should be mistress of orthodoxy, that she might not misspell, and mispronounce words so shamefully as girls usually do; and likewise that she might reprehend the true meaning of what she is saying".

A character also reveals his nature and intelligence by the kind of jokes he enjoys. In the *Nicomachean Ethics* Aristotle remarks: "There is a difference between the jesting of a free and that of a slavish man, and between that of an educated and of an uneducated person." Aristotle believes that the jokes of a gentleman are tactful, whereas a buffoon "cannot resist the temptation to be funny and spares neither himself nor others for a laugh. He says things that no cultivated man would say, and some that he would not even listen to."[13] Freud attributes the ability of making jokes to a particular talent, "a special capacity – rather in the class of the old mental 'faculties'; and it seems to emerge fairly independently of the others, such as intelligence, imagination, memory, etc." However, he does believe that the type of joke a man makes can give away his character. He mentions one of Heine's comic characters, Hirsch-Hyacinth, "a Hamburg lottery-agent, extractor of corns and professional valuer, the valet of the aristocratic Baron Cristoforo Gumpelino (formerly Gumpel)" whose jokes and jests perfectly match his personality.[14]

In comedy, the intelligent have wit, a sense of humor and the shrewdness that perceives the actual paradoxes of experience, and the agility that allows one to think on two different planes.[15] In Restoration society wit implies "intellectual superiority in perception and knowledge, and consequently, acumen, penetration, and sophistication".[16] The importance

---

[13]   *Nicomachean Ethics,* IV.8., p. 108.
[14]   Sigmund Freud, *Jokes and Their Relation to the Unconscious*, trans. James Strachey (New York: W. W. Norton, 1960), pp. 140-141.
[15]   Louis Cazamian, *The Development of English Humor* (Durham: Duke University Press, 1952), p. 6.
[16]   Thomas H. Fujimura, *The Restoration Comedy of Wit* (Princeton, N. J.: Princeton University Press, 1952), p. 19.

of being witty is amply illustrated in more recent times by the plays of Wilde and those of Shaw.

Common sense is not always the sole measure of an intelligent person. The great dreamers like Don Quixote and Cyrano, and the inhabitants of Shakespeare's Ephesus, Illyria, the forest of Arden, or Prospero's island, are not measured by down to earth common sense. Shaw remarks about the English that "they are everywhere united and made strong by their bond of their common nonsense", and their "invincible determination to tell and be told lies about everything".[17] Also, the Englishman is "firmly persuaded that his prejudices and stupidities are vital material of civilization" and, presumably, he does not feel that it is "common sense to laugh at your own prejudices; it is common sense to feel insulted when anyone else laughs at them".[18] Shaw admits that the French are different, and when we turn to Molière's plays it is obvious that excess, lack of common sense and *raison* characterize the fool. A seventeenth century French critic who comments on Molière's Tartuffe remarks: "we judge ridiculous what altogether lacks good sense."[19]

Molière's Chrysalde from *The School for Wives* cautions Arnolphe to follow the "way between extremes" which is the "proper way in which a prudent man will often stay". In the last act of *Tartuffe*, when Orgon finally is compelled to realize that he was fooled by the hypocrisy of Tartuffe, he has to listen to the admonitions of the sensible Cléante who advocates "moderation", "the path of reason", and carefully avoiding bad extremes. Arnolphe's theoretical and unrealistic approach to marriage, Orgon's blind and excessive adoration of Tartuffe, Magdelon's and Cathos' fantastic behavior adopted from the romantic novels of Madame de Scudéry, all show the characters to lack common sense and therefore cause them to become the butts of laughter. In the eighteenth century Dennis writes, "it is not Wit, but Reason and Judgement, which distinguish a man of Sense from a fool".[20] Bergson believes that "Common sense represents the endeavor of a mind continually adapting itself anew and changing ideas when it changes objects" and that

---

[17] Bernard Shaw, "Meredith on Comedy", in *Plays and Players* (London: Oxford University Press, 1955), p. 197.
[18] Shaw, "Meredith on Comedy", p. 199.
[19] Anonymous, "Letter on *The Imposter*", in Lauter, *Theories of Comedy*, p. 147.
[20] John Dennis, "A Large Account of the Taste in Poetry, and the Causes of the Degeneracy of It", in Dennis, *The Critical Works of John Dennis*, ed. Edward Niles Hooker (Baltimore: Johns Hopkins Press, 1939), Vol. I, 284.

Don Quixote who lacks this ability represents a special case, "a very special inversion of common sense".[21]

These are only some of the ways by which an author indicates that his characters possess intelligence or common sense. Man is a social being and thus all his actions and interactions with the rest of humanity reveal something significant about his nature. His inability to know and understand other people points out clearly his limitation.

Ignorance of others is not uncommon in the realm of comedy. The victims of comic plots are often unaware of the nature and motives of the practicer, who, on the other hand, knows their weaknesses and is able to deceive them. In most parent and child relationships we at times find mutual blindness and other times only the aging, foolish parents are unable to understand their offspring. A very unusual and temporary unawareness is caused by Oberon's little Western flower which blinds its victims and renders them incapable of seeing realistically the object of their love.

Besides knowing other people, man also has to be aware of his own nature. Knowledge of oneself may be the most difficult to master. That the tragic flaw is often lack of self-knowledge has been stated many times. "The tragedy of the Greeks and the Elizabethans consists typically in the failure to know oneself."[22] King Lear has "ever but slenderly known himself" and Pentheus is destroyed by Dionysus who says about him: "You do not know the limits of your strength. You do not know what you do. You do not know who you are."[23] The comic, like the tragic figure, appears often "like a sleepwalker possessed of a dreadful conceit of himself, unaware of his true nature or the world around him".[24] The lack of self-knowledge also "implies failure to recognize the nature of human limitations and this, like nearly everything else about the human condition, may occasion either tears or laughter".[25]

We even appreciate awareness of physical shortcomings and sympathize with Falstaff when he jokes about his girth and with Cyrano when he comments on his nose, but we are especially gratified when a charac-

[21] Henri Bergson, "Laughter", in *Comedy*, with George Meredith, ed. Wylie Sypher (Garden City, N. Y.: Doubleday and Co. [Anchor Books], 1956), pp. 178-179.

[22] Hoy, *The Hyacinth Room*, p. 80.

[23] Euripides, *The Bacchae*, trans. William Arrowsmith, in *Greek Tragedies*, Vol. III, eds. David Green and Richmond Lattimore (University of Chicago, 1960), p. 215.

[24] Marie Collins Swabey, *Comic Laughter* (New Haven: Yale University Press, 1961), p. 184.

[25] Hoy, *The Hyacinth Room*, p. 31.

ter is aware of deficiencies which are not so obvious. The great personages of comedy, the Millamants and Rosalinds, disarm one with their knowledge of their weaknesses whereas the Malvolios and Orgons, who are ignorant of their appearance of mental makeup, appear ludicrous to us. A special kind of attitude and behavior resulting from one's blindness to his own nature is described by Aristotle: "and generally, it is ridiculous for a man to reproach others for what he does or would do himself, or to encourage others to do what he does not or would not do himself."[26] In Sheridan's *The Rivals*, Sir Anthony, who has a vile temper, shouts at his son, "None of your passion Sir! none of your violence!. . . . Can't you be cool, like me?"

A character has to be aware not only of his own nature but also of values, of morals and ethics. Albert Cook relegates concern with ethics into the realm of tragedy and other scholars before Cook believe that moral deficiency is not a suitable subject for comedy because a "Comic play ought to represent low, trifling matter."[27] A similar argument states that a comic character is usually not judged on a moral scale, though "comedy is the natural ally of morality". It argues also that "in comedy character consists not so much in goodness or wickedness as in efficiency and inefficiency: in courage or cowardice, cleverness or stupidity, good sense or folly".[28]

However, at times knowledge of morals and ethics is essential even in the realm of comedy. Though moral codes vary from age to age, from society to society, hypocrisy, greed, and lust are vices which have not changed and have been ridiculed since the beginning of human consciousness and conscience. Amorality and unethical behavior can at times darken the mood of the play, as in *Volpone, Tartuffe,* and *Measure for Measure*, but at other times, as in Restoration Comedy, it can add sparkle to the play. Such playwrights as Shakespeare, Molière, and Jonson do not tolerate evil. Furthermore their critical attitude colors the mood of the play and the portrayal of their characters. Others, like Boccaccio and the Restoration playwrights, are more tolerant toward certain vices and the seductions and amorous adventures are not colored by censure and disapproval. Wycherly's Mrs. Pinchwife, who takes great delight in Horner's china-collection, is by no means sinister or evil.

[26] Aristotle, *The Art of Rhetoric*, trans. John Henry Friese (London: Harvard University Press, 1967; first printing, 1926), II, 23, p. 303.
[27] Marvin T. Herrick, *Comic Theory in the Sixteenth Century* (Urbana: University of Illinois Press, 1965), p. 232.
[28] Potts, *Comedy*, p. 124.

Great moral issues are less frequently subjects of comedy than are the petty, trivial problems man encounters day after day. The knowledge of manners and the ability to live up to the standards set by society are very important in the world of comedy. "The comedy of manners is the laughable born of the inability of man to conform to an artificial social standard (as in the country bumpkins), or of excessive attempts at conformity (as in the fops), or of conformity so successful that the individual loses his human elasticity (in the Bergsonian sense)."[29] Fujimura is writing about Restoration comedy when he makes these remarks; however the word "manners" covers not only the conventions of an artificial and sophisticated society, but all the efforts of man which are spent in adjusting to localized and limited ways of thinking, speaking, dressing, and behaving. While man spends his time and energy living in a socially proper way, he may lose sight of the more important issues of life and be ruled by trivialities: "the comic outlook sees the laughable incongruity in the perpetual preoccupation of men with petty questions of preferment, wealth, status as against their unmindfulness of their total contingency, their obliviousness to the brevity of life and their progress toward the grave."[30]

The "proper" way of behavior and the "right" standards and values vary from age to age, from place to place, from clique to clique. The characters of Restoration comedy try to imitate the jet set of Charles the Second, Molière's fools ape the beautiful people of Louis the Fourteenth, and Babbitt tries to adjust to the code of his country club. Some conquer the difficulties, but the less talented spend great energy adjusting to the age, the country they live in, the society, the in-group, yet they fail and remain the butts of ridicule.

The type of unawareness which is ridiculed in a comedy is important because it often sets the tone of the play and defines its complexity. Grave struggle with trivialities, with manners, results in lighthearted comedy, whereas ignorance of morals darkens the mood of a play. The most intricate works deal with people who do not know themselves and their fellow men. Not only the specific kind of unawareness which dominates the play is important but also the degree of ignorance. It is nearly impossible to determine when ignorance ceases and awareness begins, but I will attempt to divide characters into three groups: those who are ignorant, those who are partially aware, and those who know.

Among those who are unaware, one can distinguish two kinds of

29   Fujimura, *The Restoration Comedy of Wit*, p. 5.
30   Swabey, *Comic Laughter*, p. 185.

characters: those who are "natural", life-like creations, and those who are artificial beings. Great natural stupidity is difficult to portray and in doing so no one has managed to surpass Shakespeare. "I say, there is no darkness but ignorance in which thou art more puzzled than the Egyptians in their fog" says the clown to Malvolio, who lacks self-awareness and who as a butt is "plain, magnificent, unrelieved; a solemn bore, morose, and sourish to boot".[31] Bottom illustrates natural stupidity perhaps even better than does Malvolio. He exists in an un-ruffled oblivion which is "fixed and immutable, he sees neither himself nor his situation truly at any moment of the action, either before, during, or after his sojourn with immortals".[32] Evans, in his discussion of those who are ignorant and foolish, mentions not only Malvolio and Bottom but also Dogberry, Sir Andrew Aguecheek, and Caliban. He says that ". . . for the select few who dwell at Bottom's depth no device of deception is needed. The dramatist creates them as beings with insulated minds, without perception, oblivious wherever they are. They are con-genitally, chronically unaware. If Rosalind carries immunity to unaware-ness, Bottom carries one to awareness. For Rosalind, brightest of hero-ines, the dark is light enough; for bully Bottom the light is too dark, and the dark no darker."[33]

The Marquess of Halifax tries to define five orders of fools who are characterized by the "defect of ignorance". The ignorants are the "blockhead, coxcomb, vain blockhead, grave coxcomb, and the half-witted fellow".[34] Shakespeare's comic characters do not fit into pigeon-holes because they are natural, human and unique. They testify to the "genuineness of Shakespeare's psychological realism; whatever the schemes may be through which we attempt to classify the moral world, he always baffles us with hybrids, contradictory characters that overlap all categories; the reason being, of course, that he never thought of categories, but only of individuals."[35] But, since the beginnings of Greek comedy, unawareness in its various forms is often created by men who do think of categories, who stylize, distort, dehumanize the image of man, who alter nature to make follies more evident and ridiculous.

Among comic characters who are ignorant we find more who are artificial, stylized, and unnatural, than those who are human and natural.

---

[31] Cazamian, *The Development of English Humor*, p. 214.
[32] Bertrand Evans, *Shakespeare's Comedies* (Oxford: Clarendon, 1960), p. 43.
[33] *Ibid.*
[34] George Savile, "Moral Thought and Reflection", *The Complete Works of George Savile, First Marquess of Halifax* (Oxford, 1912), p. 234.
[35] Cazamian, *The Development of English Humor*, p. 216.

In the eighteenth century numerous English critics divide comedy into lower and higher types. The results of such examination yield the following observations on the nature of the natural and artificial character. Dryden differentiates between two types of plays:

Comedy consists, though of low persons, yet of natural actions and characters; I mean such humours, adventures, and designs, as are to be found and met in the world. Farce, on the other side, consists of forced humours, and unnatural events. Comedy presents us with the imperfections of human nature: Farce entertains with what is monstrous and chimerical. The one causes laughter in those who can judge of men and manners, by the lively representation of their folly or corruption: the other produces the same effect in those who can judge neither, and that only by its extravagances. The first works on the judgement and fancy; the latter on the fancy only: there is more satisfaction in the former kind of laughter, and in the latter more scorn. [36]

Dryden states also that "farce consists principally in grimaces".[37] Addison makes similar observations in *The Spectator* No. 249. "The two great Branches of Ridicule in Writing are Comedy and Burlesque, the first ridicules Persons by drawing them in their proper character, the other by drawing them quite unlike themselves."[38] Fielding says that in burlesque we find "the exhibition of what is monstrous and unnatural" and our delight arises from "the surprising absurdity as in appropriating the manners of the highest to the lowest, or *e converso*", whereas in comedy we confine ourselves "strictly to nature, from just imitation of which will flow all the pleasure we can convey to a sensible reader".[39]

All these eighteenth century writers prefer persons drawn in their "proper characters", first of all because they believe that it is much more difficult to create natural characters and, secondly, because a man of good sense prefers that which is natural. "A Comick Poet may be certain of this, that the grossest touches which are in nature, will please the men of sense, more than the most delicate strokes which are out of it."[40] Consequently writers like Congreve and Dryden have a rather low opinion of artificial characters: "Is anything more common than to have a pretended Comedy stuffed with Grotesques, Figures, and

[36]   John Dryden, Preface to "An Evening's Love", *Works*, Vol. III (Edinburgh: William Peterson, 1883), p. 241.
[37]   *Ibid.*
[38]   John Addison, *The Spectator*, No. 249 (London: George Routledge and Sons, 1757), p. 354.
[39]   Henry Fielding, *Joseph Andrews*, ed. Martin C. Battestim, rev. ed. (Boston: Houghton Mifflin, 1961), Author's preface, p. 8.

Farce Fools? Things that are not in Nature, or if they are, are Monsters and Birth of Mischance."[41] Dryden, for the same reason, has misgivings about the contemporary French theatre, "for their poets, wanting judgement to make or maintain true characters, strive to cover their defects with ridiculous figures and grimaces".[42]

Is the play actually better when it is populated with natural characters or artificial ones? A master can create artificial characters and write as good a comedy as one who presents human characters, but the less skillful dramatist is likely to be forgotten more easily if he populates his play with types and caricatures. Edith Hamilton feels that the predilection for type or lifelike character depends on the age one lives in and also on the nationality of the writer. "In modern days the art which is inclined toward the typical, which is centered in what the mind and eye perceive, is best exemplified by the French. The individualizing tendency, the preoccupation with the deep and lonely life of each human being marks the English. The French are interested in what things are; the English in what things mean. They are the great poets of the modern world and the French are the great intellectuals."[43]

When the Frenchman, Henri Bergson, writes about comedy he discusses the artificial and mechanical characters. And, to this group, the ignorant ones who are not lifelike, belong the "early Molière characters the *précieuses*, the Sganarelles", also the "later Bélise, Orgon, and Monsieur Jourdain" who are "wholly unaware. Their perception of themselves and of others never coincides with that of the spectator. Whoever pulls the strings easily manipulates them. Their comedy is candid and mechanical."[44]

The grouping of these artificial characters will be always somewhat arbitrary, but most of them can be contained in the following four categories: caricatures, humor characters, morality characters, and types. Their physical and mental shortcomings are usually conveyed by the exaggeration of the negative traits; lack of reason is indicated by folly in excess and lack of tact by gross blunders.

[40] Dennis, *The Critical Works of John Dennis*, p. 282.
[41] William Congreve, "Concerning Humour in Comedy", *Comedies*, ed. Bonamy Dobrée (London: Oxford University Press, 1966; first printing 1925), p. 3.
[42] Dryden, "An Evening's Love", p. 242.
[43] Edith Hamilton, *The Greek Way* (New York: Mentor Book Publ., The New American Library, 1960; first printing, 1948), p. 240.
[44] Ramon Fernandez, "The Comedy of Will", in Molière, *A Collection of Critical Essays*, ed. Jacques Guicharnaud (Englewood Cliffs, N. J.: Prentice Hall, 1964), p. 51.

Caricature is a ludicrous and grotesque representation of man's most characteristic features. Fielding defines caricature first as it is used in painting: ". . . its aim is to exhibit monsters, not men, and all distortions and exaggerations whatever are within its proper province. Now, what *Caricatura* is in painting, Burlesque is in writing; and in the same manner the comic writer and painter correlate to each other."[45] Fielding deplores the use of caricature; Paul Gaultier, a Frenchman, on the other hand, highly appreciates this method of depicting character. For him, the most accusatory caricatures are the most laughable. The only cause of laughter is the exaggeration of the ugly, but ugliness is not sought for its own sake but to show up the ideal by contrast. Caricature is *"la protestation de ce qui devrait être contre ce que est."*[46]

Caricature is considered to be a method of comic presentation which humiliates personages, but at times does not seem to degrade the object it depicts. The caricatures of favorite public figures are more complimentary than derogatory and often those are parodied who are dear to the public.

A humor character is dehumanized and distorted in the same way as caricatures are but there may be no living model after whom the image is shaped. Also, the traits which are ridiculed are better defined than are those of a caricature. The excess deals with moods and fancy exhibited in fantastic and odd actions and thoughts. In *Everyman out of his Humour,* Jonson clearly defines the nature of humor in the prologue:

> As when some one peculiar quality
> Doth so possess a man that it doth draw
> All his affects, his spirit, and his powers,
> In their confluxions, all to run one way,
> This may be truly said to be a humour.

In humor characters we are presented with the exaggeration of mental dispositions and inclinations which usually point out lack of reason and good sense. Traherne mentions in his *Christian Ethics*: "A wise man discards the predominancy of all humour . . . for he is to live the life of reason, not of humour."[47]

In the twentieth century Cazamian remarks that "Jonson's war is

---

[45]   Swabey, *Comic Laughter*, p. 40.
[46]   Paul Gaultier, "Le rire et la caricature", in J. Y. T. Greig, *The Psychology of Laughter and Comedy* (New York: Dodd, Mead and Company, 1923), p. 273.
[47]   Thomas Traherne, *Christian Ethics* (Ithaca, N. Y.: Cornell University Press, 1968), p. 175.

now against unconscious excess, in the name of sanity and balance, and now against a kind of social vanity that corrupts the whole being for the sake of a silly gratification."[48] According to Lauter, Jonson recognizes the "compulsive, mechanical nature of humour-bound characters" and by presenting them on the stage tries to free men "from the domination of such ludicrous rigidity".[49] One finds not only those who hold positive and complimentary views about humor characters but also critics who object to the use of these artificial characters. "It is often said that the comedy of Humours is by nature unimaginative: that it classifies people into types and invents appropriate speeches and actions for them but never brings them to life – that is to say it does not conceive them as complete human beings."[50]

The artificiality of a humor character depends on the exaggeration of a "peculiar quality" whereas the unnatural quality of type relies on the use of oversimplification and repetition. According to Bergson "a really living life should never repeat itself. Wherever there is repetition or complete similarity, we always suspect some mechanism at work behind the living."[51] Not only the mechanical quality is ridiculous but also "Simplified generalities are much easier to group and 'rib' than individuals in their rich complexity."[52] Some critics believe that only human life in all its freshness, diversity, provocativeness of meaning offers the greatest possibility of the ludicrous. Therefore they delegate the repetitious type into the realm of low comedy as Fujimura does. In his book on Restoration comedy he argues that the "writers of wit comedy presented the Truewit realistically", but the lower characters, the affected coxcomb, the superannuated coquette and others, are presented as types.[53] Edith Hamilton, on the other hand, believes that "type belongs to comedy, intellectual comedy, the comedy of wit and satire".[54]

The fourth category of artificial characters consists of the morality, or as Bergson calls them, vice characters. Abstract ideas are personified in the vice figure of the Middle Ages, a character who appears in various disguises in sixteenth and seventeenth century English comedies. Avarice, greed, hypocrisy are portayed in Molière's comedies, and in

---

[48] Cazamian, *Development of English Humour*, p. 314.
[49] Lauter, *Theories of Comedy*, p. 112.
[50] Potts, *Comedy*, p. 121.
[51] Bergson, "Laughter", *Comedy*, p. 82.
[52] Swabey, *Comic Laughter*, p. 34.
[53] Fujimura, *The Restoration Comedy of Wit*, p. 54.
[54] Hamilton, *The Greek Way*, p. 239.

our age, which like the Middle Ages tends toward abstractions, boredom, futility, and aimlessness walk the boards in human shapes.

Since the beginnings of literary criticism the artificial, stylized characters had been the main concern of those who wrote about comedy. Aristotle's comedy is "... an imitation of characters of a lower type — not, however, in the full sense of the word bad, the Ludicrous being merely the subdivision of the ugly. It consists in some defect or ugliness which is not painful or destructive. To take an obvious example, the comic mask is ugly and distorted, but does not imply pain."[55] Dryden's remark that farce consist mainly of "grimaces" echoes Aristotle's concept of the distorted appearance of the comic personage. Cicero also asserts that the comic character is in some way deformed[56] and that laughter is stimulated by satirizing the characters of others.[57]

During the Renaissance the Italian and French critics follow in the footsteps of Aristotle and Cicero. These men read the plays of Menander, Plautus and Terence and watched the performance of the early Renaissance farces which mainly utilized types and caricatures. It is curious, though, that Bergson, in the late nineteenth century, should mainly be concerned with this group of characters. He states that "every comic character is a type" and that the object of high-class comedy is to depict types.[58] Bergson's comic character is inflexible, artificial, mechanical, and rigid, and he defines rigidity as "the neglect to look around — and more especially within oneself".[59] Lauter points out the kinship between the classical theories and Bergson's ideas when he makes the observation that "rigidity replaces the ancient *turpitudo,* baseness, ugliness, or lowness, as the essence of the ridiculous".[60]

Yet, there were those who found these definitions of comic character unsatisfactory. Maggi and Castelvetro tried to modify Aristotle's ideas and, in England, Fielding voiced his disapproval without mincing when he said: "Aristotle, who is so fond and free of definitions, hath not thought proper to define the ridiculous."[61] The objection to Bergson's

---

[55] Aristotle, *Poetics*, V., p. 21.
[56] Cicero, *De Oratore*, trans. E. W. Sutton (London: Harvard University Press, 1967, first printing, 1942), II., p. 375.
[57] *De Oratore*, p. 385.
[58] Bergson, "Laughter", *Comedy*, pp. 156-157.
[59] "Laughter", p. 156.
[60] Lauter, *Theories of Comedy*, p. 376.
[61] Fielding, *Joseph Andrews*, p. 10.

theory is that it applies only to "clowns, buffoons, to the patter and gestures of stock funnymen in the theatre", that a

... character like Falstaff is not mechanical in his behavior or mental processes; nor is Tom Sawyer, the "Duke," or Huckleberry Finn. Certainly the sly villains, gamblers, and con men of O. Henry show no lack of suppleness, nimbleness, or want of awareness of themselves or of life. Far from being dull, inert, repetitious stereotypes, these gentle grafters are alert, unpredictable, swift as lightning. What makes us laugh at them is their not letting their right hand know what their left hand doeth, the disparity between their lofty speeches and low behavior, their cockeyed views of the world. [62]

Dissatisfaction with rigidity and *turpitudo* as comic is also voiced by those critics who analyze the natural, flexible characters. As these commentators examine the personages of Boccaccio, Fielding, Cervantes, and Meredith, they discover that comic characters do not have to be types, they do not have to be rigid, deformed, or, even ignorant.

Indeed, many of the great comic characters are flexible, unique, often intelligent and at least partially aware of their own nature, of others, and the ways of the world. It is difficult to determine which characters are ignorant and which are partially aware. If a person becomes aware of his specific folly, he can either eliminate the fault or consciously indulge in it, in which case he becomes an eccentric. One often approves of an eccentric because he dares to follow his inclinations, whereas we laugh at those who are not conscious of their faults and are blindly victimized by their shortcomings. Members of this group usually take the middle position in comedy; they are capable of gulling the ignorant, but since their awareness is not on the level of the "knowing", they themselves can easily become the butts of laughter. The partially aware cannot always be considered comic characters because at times we laugh with them and not at them, and frequently we identify ourselves completely with their trials and even their deficiencies.

Nearly all men consist of a blend of awareness and ignorance which enables them to gain insight at times but also renders them capable of being ridiculous if they sometimes happen to be unable to perceive matters of importance. The great comic characters of Boccaccio, Chaucer, Shakespeare, and others fall into this category. Shakespeare is most often mentioned in literary criticism as a writer who created life-like characters. "Shakespeare's instinct seems very early to have felt that fools were much more satisfactory in every way if they were

[62] Swabey, *Comic Laughter*, pp. 37-38.

conscious, even dimly and by glimpses, of their foolishness."[63] In his plays "complete hidebound dunces are not many; more frequent everywhere, and chiefly among rustics, are the semi-dunces partly alive to the true state of things, including themselves. The flavor of rusticity in all lands is largely made up of that mixture of naivete, ignorance, and sly, half-shrewd awareness."[64] In Shakespeare's plays "unique characters take hand in the plot and are themselves the source of fun".[65]

Inevitably it is Falstaff who is mentioned as the most versatile and flexible comic character Shakespeare created. "A stupid Butt is only fit for the conversation of ordinary people: men of wit require one that will give them play, and bestir himself in the absurd part of his behavior. A butt with these accomplishments frequently gets the laugh on his side, and turns the ridicule upon him that attacks him. Sir John Falstaff was an hero of this species."[66] Falstaff is intelligent, resourceful, ingenious; he is conscious not only of his physical appearance but also his mental makeup. He has "shrewd control over himself which the rogue manages to keep all the time; with his watching and letting himself go only as far as he likes; with the cool judgement which adds a flavor of self-mockery to the absurdity of his pranks."[67] But, there is a limit to Falstaff's vision and knowledge: "the old man who shows such insight into the character of Shallow, for instance, loses all his penetration wherever his Prince is concerned."[68]

Various characteristics of those who are partially aware are discussed as early as the seventeenth century. Congreve recognizes that inflexibility and, as he call it, "gross folly" are not necessarily prerequisities for making a personage ridiculous; and, as do many of the later writers, he tries to find a substitute for "natural folly (which is incorrigible, and therefore not proper for the stage)".[69] Congreve depicts "affected wit", and Fielding makes fun of affectations and pretensions. They shift from attempts to define the whole nature of a comic character to the discussion of a certain trait that makes man ridiculous. Some authors realize that individuality and even greatness do not exclude the possibility of the comic. Bernard Schilling states that "Pope saw that

[63] Cazamian, *The Development of English Humour*, p. 197.
[64] *Ibid.*
[65] Swabey, *Comic Laughter*, p. 149.
[66] Addison, *Spectator*, No. 47, p. 79.
[67] Cazamian, *The Development of English Humor*, p. 251.
[68] Cazamian, p. 251.
[69] William Congreve, "Dedication", *The Way of the World* in *Complete Plays*, p. 336.

human beings are ridiculous and great at once, that the more dignity and responsibility they have, the greater is their potentiality to be absurd", and that Addison realized that even fools can have "proper character".[70] Dr. Johnson remarks that "to raise mirth, it is by no means universally necessary that the personages should be either mean or corrupt".[71]

In the nineteenth century Meredith attempts to draw a more comprehensive picture of life-like characters. He examines, among others, the personages of Molière and Shakespeare. Bergson, who turned to Molière's plays for inspiration and illustration for his theory, sees in the French playwright's characters magnificent but artificial creations. Meredith, who reexamines these men, finds that they are not only abstract, general types, "humorous exaggerations", but that they are very much alive and as he calls them, "permanently human".[72] Meredith also observes Shakespeare's comic characters and says that they are "saturated with the comic spirit; with more of what we call blood-life than is to be found anywhere out of Shakespeare; and they are of this world, but they are of the world enlarged to our embrace by imagination, and by great poetic imagination".[73]

The third group deals with those who know, who are aware of themselves, of manners, morals and the way of the world. This group may be divided into three categories; to the first belong those who know but are unable to live up to certain standards; to the second, those who know but are unwilling to conform; and to the third belong those who are aware of that which is right and live up to the ideal standards.

Those who are aware and select the wrong way are usually complex characters, both in tragedy and comedy. Maggi tries to explain why man makes the wrong choices. "Wrong appetite" wins over reason resulting in a kind of ignorance, "the ignorance of a deformed disposition is that which is formed of deformed ratiocination".[74] A frequently used comic device which one can call "deformed ratiocination" is rationalization to achieve ends which are not altogether acceptable. After Boccaccio's Abbott discovers one of his monks dallying with a pretty peasant girl, instead of punishing the culprit, he does as the monk did. But before he frolics with the girl he rationalizes, "Truly, why shouldn't I take

---

[70] Bernard N. Schilling, *Comic Spirit: Boccaccio to Thomas Mann* (Detroit: Wayne University Press, 1965), p. 15.
[71] Samuel Johnson, *The Rambler*, No. 125 (London: Dove, 1827), p. 109.
[72] George Meredith, "An Essay on Comedy", *Comedy*, with Henri Bergson, p. 14.
[73] "An Essay on Comedy", p. 16.
[74] Maggi, "On the Ridiculous", *Theories of Comedy*, by Paul Lauter, p. 68.

my pleasure when I can? Sorrow and annoyance for that matter are always ready, whether I want them or not. .... And a sin that is hidden is half shriven. The opportunity may not come to me again and it is the best sort of wisdom to take advantage of a bounty when the Lord God sees fit to send it."[75] The Wife of Bath similarly explains the weakness of the flesh:

> Myn ascendent was Taur, and Mars therinne.
> Allas! Allas! that evere love was sinne!
> I folwed ay myn inclinacioun
> By vertu of myn constellacioun.

Since Aristotle authors have been aware that the discrepancy between what is and what ought to be is often the source of tragedy and comedy. Aristotle discusses those who are "wrong both in what they say and in the advice they give", because "either through want of sense they form incorrect opinions, or, if their opinions are correct, through viciousness they do not say what they think, or, if they are sensible and good, they lack goodwill; wherefore it may happen that they do not give the best advice, although they know what it is."[76] Alfred Michiels states that discrepancy creates laughter; "*Tout ce qui est contraire à l'idéal absolue de la perfection humaine excite le rire et produit un effect comique.*"[77] Mme. de Staël applies the idea to eighteenth-century satire: "*Swift, dans Gulliver et le conte du Tonneau, de même que Voltaire dans ses écrits philosophiques, tire des plaisanteries très heureuses de l'opposition qui existe entre l'erreur reçue et la vérité proscrite, entre les institutions et la nature des choses.*"[78] All great writers who are aware of man's frailty are alert as Boccaccio is "to men who say one thing and actually do in their weakness something quite different".[79]

In a recently published book, *The Hyacinth Room*, Cyrus Hoy examines those tragic, tragicomic and comic characters who seek to fashion their behavior according to an ideal conduct, but fail. In this case,

... the dramatic protagonist is endowed with the rational and critical faculties which enable him to discern, no less than the audience, which witnesses the spectacle of his fall, the destruction to which he is inexorably

---

[75]   Boccaccio, *The Decameron*, I.4., p. 20.
[76]   Aristotle, *Rhetoric*, II.1., p. 171.
[77]   Alfred Michiels, "Essai sur le talent de Regnard et sur le talent comique en général", in *Œuvres complètes de Regnard* (Paris: Adolphe Delahays, 1859), p. 3.
[78]   Holstein Staël, Anne Louise Germaine, *De la littérature*, ed. Paul van Tieghem, 2 vols. (Genève: Droz, 1958), Vol. II, p. 216.
[79]   Schilling, *Comic Spirit: Boccaccio to Thomas Mann*, p. 23.

driven, even as he moves along his disastrous way. The effect of this is to increase inestimably the uses of irony for both tragedy and comedy, for the psychological ambivalences which irony brings into focus, project in a simple, incongruous image the grandeur to which man aspires and the degradation to which he is perversely driven. [80]

In tragedy this is the realm of Phaedra and in comedy the Widow of Ephesus would be the counterpart.

Plato would place these characters among the partially aware. He would argue that their behavior is due to a kind of ignorance, because no one who really knows what is good and right, would decide to follow the wrong way. Hoy suggests that this kind of behavior is a kind of unawareness of self when he remarks that these comic personages seem to be "bemused at the contradiction which their natures exhibit". They wonder why "they should be endowed with such rational clarity concerning their path, and yet be so irresistibly drawn to the wrong one". [81]

We can forgive evil committed in ignorance, we can sympathize with those who know, but are unable to do the right thing, but wickedness committed with complete awareness is seldom excusable. To this category belong those who are aware but unwilling to live up to the ideal, the villains and evil practicers who are consciously bent on hurting and ruining their fellow men. Even triumphant evil can be at times amusing. Some of the practicers of Jacobean and Restoration comedy, who are bent not on correcting, but corrupting their fellow men, belong to this group. Subtle of Jonson's *The Alchemist* and Horner of Wycherly's *The Country Wife* remain unpunished. Other times, though, order is restored by a superior, and usually benevolent power. Sometimes this power is represented by a more acceptable moral behavior as in *The Second Shepherd's Play*, when Mak is subdued and tossed in a blanket by the three shepherds who are more honest than he is. At other times order is restored by a symbol of higher justice: the court, the king, or God. Volpone is punished severely by the court of justice, and Tartuffe is taken captive by the French king. One can certainly argue that these characters belong to the realm of the partially aware and that the superior power represents greater knowledge which discovers evil and restores order to the universe. Not too many comic characters belong to this group and the next one, which consists of those who are aware and live up to ideals.

[80] Hoy, *The Hyacinth Room*, p. 232.
[81] *The Hyacinth Room*, p. 200.

Among those who are aware and use their knowledge for the best we find the benevolent practicers, the Oberons, the Prosperos, and also those who do not direct any action, but set a standard of conduct in the play. These are not ridiculous, but occasionally we find a comic character in this group, as at times even perfection can be ridiculous. Barrie's remarkable Crichton and Woodhouse's absolutely perfect Jeeves are people who meticulously live up to the code of their profession and that of their social class. But, one can argue that their portrayal comes dangerously close to being caricature, a comic exaggeration of perfection, and that they do not belong to this category.

In the last part of this essay some remarks have to be made about the nature of the comic character and the reader's and audience's reaction toward him. As Bergson remarks: "The chief cause of rigidity is the neglect to look around – and more especially within oneself."[82] Also, "The comic person is unconscious. As though wearing the ring of Gyges with reverse effect, he becomes invisible to himself while remaining visible to all the world."[83] Yet, one of Bergson's statements on this topic is rather unacceptable. He says that the comic character is "generally comic in proportion to his ignorance of himself". This is most of the time true for plays which employ artificial characters but not always applicable to those which are populated with "natural" people. Bottom who is quite unaware is not funnier than Falstaff. A more valid statement pertains also to the degree of awareness. "The degree to which a comic hero is aware of what makes him funny determines his level on the human ladder."[84] The benevolent, and at times also the evil practicers are supremely aware and in control of the rest of the characters in the play.

There is another problem in connection with comic character which is more frequently discussed than degree of ignorance: is a comic character capable of development and does he remain comic after he becomes aware of his faults? Those who are very ignorant usually remain unchanged. There does not seem to be much hope for the Malvolios, Mascarilles, and Orgons. Even if Orgon manages to discover that Tartuffe is evil, one has the feeling that the moment another Tartuffe comes along, he'll behave with as much inflexible stupidity as he did

[82]   Bergson, "Laughter", *Comedy*, p. 156.
[83]   Bergson, *Comedy*, p. 71.
[84]   Fernandez, "The Comedy of Will", *Molière, A Collection of Critical Essays*, p. 51.

before. With the ignorant the learning process, if there is any, is seldom convincing; insight is delayed to the last moments of the play when, after punishment and ridicule, the character miraculously reforms.

It is different with those who are partially aware. Great comedy "ends with the restoration of the individual to himself, and to all that, in the widest sense, can be said to give him his identity. He will have lost it, if he ever has it, through sundry transgressions, follies and inconsistencies; also through the force of the sundry delusions which he has entertained, and which keep him from knowing himself and his proper good."[85] The knowledge of one's true character and one's proper good is, according to Hoy, "not the least marvels which comedy celebrates".[86] Northrop Frye believes that not only the insight itself but also the degree to which a character is enlightened about his faults and the way he is corrected are of importance. In comedy "the blocking characters are more often reconciled or converted than simply repudiated. Comedy often includes a scapegoat ritual expulsion which gets rid of some irreconcilable characters, but exposure and disgrace make for pathos, or even tragedy."[87] Frye mentions *Volpone,* which "ends with a great bustle of sentences to penal servitude and the galleys, and one feels that the deliverance of society hardly needs so much hard labor".[88] Also, at times man can't face the whole truth about his own nature. If he is suddenly stripped of all his defenses and is mercilessly told about his shortcomings and frailties, the play might end in tragedy. "In the world of comedy, to take away a man's delusions is to assist him toward the sort of self-knowledge out of which true happiness springs; to take away his illusions is to deprive him of the protective shield that stands between him and reality."[89]

In comedy characters are more often static than in tragedy because, as it has been stated since Aristotle, comedy is frequently populated with "low" and ignorant people who are inflexible and do not have the potentiality for change and development. But in the great plays of Shakespeare and Shaw man often achieves insight and becomes aware of the true nature of things. "From the first comedies Shakespeare has concentrated exploitative efforts upon two great moments, that in which

[85] Hoy, *The Hyacinth Room*, p. 312.
[86] *Ibid.*
[87] Northrop Frye, *Anatomy of Criticism* (Princeton, N. J.: Princeton University Press, 1957), p. 165.
[88] *Ibid.*
[89] Hoy, *The Hyacinth Room*, pp. 113-114.

ignorance has achieved greatest depth and universality, and that in which persons who have acted in ignorance learn their errors."[90]

The process of growth and development is a gratifying experience, although a character ceases to be comic after he gains insight. Eliza Doolittle learns quickly and her transformation is eminently successful. She has to learn manners but Candide's problem is much more complex. He has to learn to think, to form a philosophy of life and he has to achieve wisdom. Candide is a slow learner, and he is wonderfully ridiculous as long as he does not think for himself but unquestioningly accepts Pangloss' illogical philosophy, as long as he nurses his delusions, fails to recognize the true nature of people and is unaware of the way of the world. But, from the moment he begins to think, faces the fact that Cunegonde is neither good nor beautiful, that Pangloss is a fool and happiness is not to be found necessarily in Paraguay, France, or even in Westphalia, he ceases to be a comic character.

Occasionally it is left to the reader to decide if a character is capable of learning. Such is the case of Jonah. He knows that God is "merciful, slow to anger, of great kindness and willing to forgive evil", but he fails to notice the shortcomings of his own nature. Even after his confinement in the belly of the great fish he does not realize that he is far from being merciful. He keeps a vengeful vigil in the desert hoping that the Ninevites will perish. At the very end of the story we still do not find out whether Jonah is capable of insight or not. Will he remain a blind and static character until the end of his days? The question is raised but not answered.

The audience and the reader often react strongly to comic character and it is always interesting to observe such responses. Our laughter does not only reveal much about ourselves but helps us define the nature of a comic personage. Because of the close relationship between presentation and reaction, theories of comedy and theories of laughter are nearly inseparable, and one is seldom discussed without the other. In *Love's Labour Lost* Rosaline says: "A jest's prosperity lies in the ear of him that hears it, never in the tongue of him that makes it."

The nature of laughter depends first of all on our individual perception and attitudes. There are countless influences which shape our sense of humor and our reaction to the ludicrous. Certain kinds of humor can not travel beyond the boundaries of a country and "civilized society

[90]   Evans, *Shakespeare's Comedies*, p. 288.

discourages cruel jokes and brutal laughter".[91] Addison suggests that our reaction is influenced by education: "In proportion as one man is more refined than another, he chuses his fool out of a lower or higher class of mankind."[92] While Addison attributes man's appreciation of low comic characters to his lack of education, Max Eastman tries to show that enjoyment of derisive humor is associated with the possession of egocentric, individualistic, aggressive and world-derogatory sentiment, and, if one enjoys crude disparaging jokes, it is an indication of "repressed malice, that is, of an unconscious need for destruction".[93] Unquestionably the emotional makeup of a person has a decisive influence on his reaction to that which is comic. Those who are deeply compassionate laugh less at Don Quixote, Charley Chaplin and other characters who are a mixture of the ridiculous and the pathetic than do those who feel less and perceive with their intellect. One could go on *ad infinitum* to prove why various people perceive the comic in different ways.

Besides our personal attitudes, our reaction to the character depends on the way a ridiculous person is presented to us. Some great writers are aware of the shortcomings of humanity, yet are able to accept and love man with all his foibles and vices. Bernard Schilling, who discusses the works of such authors in *The Comic Spirit,* feels that laughter is tempered by sympathy when one encounters the characters created by writers such as Boccaccio, Fielding and Thomas Mann. These authors observe man with all his foibles and weaknesses yet love him and accept him, whereas the creations of the satirist reflect the harsh rejection and criticism of humanity. Potts feels though that a comic character must not "seem to us heroic" and should invite "critical judgement rather than arouse strongly sympathetic feeling". He should not evoke "strongly antipathetic feelings either".[94]

Our laughter is also conditioned by the range and complexity of responses we experience when we encounter a person. One can generalize that we laugh at those who are ignorant, and that we laugh with those who know. The reader's reaction is not so simple when he meets those who are partially aware. We laugh at Falstaff because he is portly, we laugh at him when he becomes the victim of a plot, but we laugh

[91] W. K. Wimsatt, *English Stage Comedy*, ed. and intro. W. K. Wimsatt (New York: Columbia University Press, 1955), p. 8.
[92] Addison, *Spectator*, No. 47, p. 79.
[93] Max Eastman, *Enjoyment of Laughter* (New York: Simon and Schuster, 1936), p. 352.
[94] Potts, *Comedy*, p. 116.

with him when he is the victimizer, when his sharp insights allow him and us to recognize the foibles of others; and, to complicate matters, we laugh with him at his own deficiencies. The shifting, from one attitude to another, gives variety and involves the reader with the character. Such change of attitude would seem nonsensical to Bergson and others who believe that one remains at a distance from the comic personage and that absence of feeling accompanies the laughable.

Two main trends are discernible when one examines the theories of laughter: the advocates of derisive laughter who believe that amusement is an expression of contempt and there are those who feel that laughter can be sympathetic and benevolent.

To the first group, which is the larger one, belong those who think that the reader feels superior to the comic character and enjoys seeing him ridiculed. "Witless and Witwoud are ridiculous because of a defect, intellectual, social and aesthetic; and in laughing at them we feel a sense of 'sudden glory'."[95] When Feibleman discusses Hobbes' theory of laughter he remarks that it is a little milder, a "little more subjectively expressed than Aristotle's but essentially they are the same".[96] Both believe that laughter is derisive. Bergson states that laughter is "above all corrective. Being intended to humiliate, it must make a painful impression on the person against whom it is directed. By laughter, society avenges itself for the liberties taken with it. It would fail in its object if it bore the stamp of sympathy and kindness."[97] It does not seem to be a coincidence that those critics who believe that laughter is derisive are the ones who in their theories on comic character consider only personages who belong to the group of the artificial, the unnatural fools.

Those who on the other hand are concerned with the partially aware and assert that a person can be ridiculous even if he is flexible and life-like, most often believe that laughter can be benevolent. Congreve, who creates characters who are alive and charming, objects to cruel laughter at innate physical and mental deficiencies. In the nineteenth century, Charles Lamb is aware of the foibles of mankind, yet his laughter is kind and benevolent, and Carlyle in defining true humor states that it is "not contempt, its essence is love".[98]

The assertion which is made by Bergson and others that we feel no

---

[95] Fujimura, *The Restoration Comedy of Wit*, p. 67.
[96] James Feibleman, *In Praise of Comedy* (London: Russel, 1939), p. 97.
[97] Bergson, "Laughter", *Comedy*, p. 187.
[98] Thomas Carlyle, "Essay on Jean Paul Richter", *Critical and Miscellaneous Essays*, Vol. I (Chicago: Belford, Clarke, 1880), p. 130.

emotion toward comic characters, except disparagement, is contradicted by those who believe that laughter can be sympathetic. Plato recognized that comedy evokes often a mixture of pleasure and pain, and also others argue that laughter can be fused with sorrow, sympathy, pity, and compassion. "Thurber is a living disproof of Bergson's assertion that laughter is incompatible with emotion",[99] says Eastman.

It is possible to explain contradictory thoughts on the nature of the comic character by describing the kind of person the author had in mind when he composed his theory. Also it is possible to show why people react in such diverse ways to those who are ridiculous. Man consciously or unconsciously compares himself with the characters on the stage. Addison states that the "secret elation and pride of heart what is generally called laughter" arises in man "from his comparing himself with an object below him, whether it so happens that it be a natural or an artificial fool".[100] A contemporary of Molière's feels that we are contemptuous of those who lack reason and good sense. "Now, this contempt is a relative sentiment, like every kind of pride; that is to say, it consists in a comparison of the despised object with ourselves to the disadvantage of their person in whom we see this lack of good sense and to our advantage. For, when we see a ridiculous action, our knowledge of the folly of this action raises us above the one who performs it because, on the one hand since no one consciously behaves unreasonably, we assume that the person involved does not know it to be unreasonable, and believes it to be reasonable."[101]

The result is that we are pleased to have perceived the error and feel superior in our knowledge. Freud recognizes that we compare ourselves not only with those who are fools and are inferior to us, but also with those who are superior. "A person appears comic to us if, in comparison with ourselves he makes too great an expenditure of his bodily function and too little of his mental ones; and it cannot be denied that in both these cases our laughter expresses a pleasurable sense of the superiority which we feel in relation to him. If the relation in the two cases is reversed − if the other person's physical expenditure is found to be less than ours or his mental expenditure greater − then we no longer laugh, we are filled with astonishment and admiration."[102]

If we compare ourselves with those who are ignorant and especially

[99]   Eastman, *Enjoyment of Laughter*, p. 87.
[100] Addison, *Spectator*, No. 47, p. 79.
[101] Anonymous, "Letter on *The Imposter*", in Lauter, *Theories of Comedy*, p. 152.
[102] Freud, *Jokes and Their Relation to the Unconcious*, pp. 195-196.

with the artificial characters, we do feel superior and feel little or no emotion when they are the butts of ridicule. These characters are less aware than we are, and are also removed from the realm of humans. Their artificiality, deformity, mechanistic behavior make identification with them unlikely and, as Bergson would say, they become "things" which have no kinship with our existence. If, on the other hand, we encounter characters who are partially aware, our reaction toward them will be completely different. Identification with them is possible. We all have those dark hours when we walk around with an ass's head on our shoulders and are unaware of ourselves and the world around us, and we have at times those rare moments in life when we are Oberons, Rosalinds, and Millamants, wonderfully aware and in control of everything, but usually we live in a precarious state of semi-awareness, ready to become the victims of our limited vision. We perceive the same qualities in the character of Parson Adams, Walter Mitty, Don Camillo, and as we are able to identify with them our laughter is tempered by sympathy and understanding. Meredith remarks that "heart and mind laugh out at Don Quixote".[103]

When we encounter the rogues and villains we return to a rather complex version of the "superiority" reaction combined with identification and what Monro calls "release from restraint". Those who sometimes enjoy being wicked identify themselves with the practicer and enjoy gulling those who are ignorant. Presumably the experience is a kind of catharsis, a vicarious experience of being pleasingly nefarious which cleanses the participant from his aggressions and frees him from inhibitions. Identification usually ceases when the practicer is overpowered and the reader righteously sides with the just, benevolent, victorious power. The reaction of those who do not enjoy being wicked must be rather simple. Comparison with the villain would result in a sense of superiority, a feeling of contempt, and "sudden glory" when the rogue is punished.

It is rare though that a man should be so righteous as to feel unadulterated contempt for those who know and are unable to live up to an ideal conduct. Again, the process of comparison is likely to result in identification and benevolent laughter, or at least some emotion other than contempt. "In its treatment of reason overthrown, comedy makes it clear just how vulnerable human dignity is and by implication, how

[103] George Meredith, "Prelude", The Egoist, ed. Lionel Stevenson (Boston: Houghton Mifflin, 1958), p. 77.

susceptible all efforts at rationality are to the potent beast that lurks within."[104]

Those who know and do live up to an ideal standard are rarely comic characters but we still compare ourselves with them. They warrant, as Freud said, our admiration and if we are taken into their confidence and direct with them those who know less, we are flattered. If they make fools of themselves to entertain and amuse other people, our laughter is mingled with admiration. "The feeling of superiority does not arise in the other person if he knows that one has only been pretending; and this affords fresh evidence of the fundamental independence of the comic from the feeling of superiority."[105]

Attempts to categorize anything, laughter, awareness, comic character, can never be completely satisfactory. Especially in comedy, which is so elusive and has such infinite variety, one can find innumerable exceptions to any rule. Dr. Johnson remarks that "Comedy has been particularly unpropitious to definers."[106]

The manifold contradictions found in the theories concerning comedy, and particularly in the theories on comic character, make it difficult to find an all-inclusive approach. The contradictions arise often because the author of a theory has not specified the kind of comic character he attempted to define. Aristotle's concept that a comic personage is necessarily ugly and Bergson's rigidity theory can successfully be applied to the artificial, ignorant fools but these ideas fail to be valid when one considers the life-like dunces of Shakespeare. Similarly, Meredith's and Schilling's statements regarding semi-aware and frequently highly sympathetic characters do not apply when one considers the simple and mechanical types and caricatures.

The ignorance-awareness chain established in this essay suggests that perhaps contradictory theories on comic characters can be regarded in a new light and they might even be reconciled with each other. They cease to be inconsistent if one considers them as not covering the whole range of comic personages but only a segment of them. The same is true for the seemingly incongruous statementst made on the nature of laughter and the audience's reaction to a comic character.

The ignorance-awareness chain of comic beings, suggested since Plato but never before consciously developed, is limited and deficient in many ways. It is by no means all inclusive and one can find comic

[104] Hoy, *The Hyacinth Room*, p. 192.
[105] Freud, *Jokes and Their Relation to the Unconscious*, p. 199.
[106] Samuel Johnson, *The Rambler*, No. 122, p. 102.

characters which do not fit readily into this system. But, it is an approach which makes it frequently possible to discover the source of the ludicrous in a fool and it enables the reader to explore the comic possibilities of ignorance in its endless variations.

II

DEGREES OF IGNORANCE AND KNOWLEDGE

THE TWILIGHT OF THE MIND: CARICATURE

Buckingham's *The Rehearsal* presents an "all embracing burlesque"[1] of the heroic rhyming play of the Restoration period. The author censures the contrived plots, the bombastic speeches, the artificial characters of such dramas. He also frequently parodies the creations of his contemporary playwrights, Dryden, Davenant, Howard, Killigrew, and Behn. The central character of *The Rehearsal* is Bayes, the poet, who is not only the epitome of the bad writer but also a vicious personal caricature. He is one of the great, ignorant and artificial characters of the age, often alluded to by Restoration writers. Montague Summers mentions that he is a "composite figure" and that "it was not until the brilliant successes of *Tyrannic Love* and *The Conquest of Granada* in 1669 and 1670 that Buckingham concentrated upon Dryden as the chief butt, the traits of the four Howards, Davenant, and other dramatists being worked in with telling and distinct, although subsidiary touches".[2] Before the first performance of the play Buckingham personally instructed the comedian who played the role of Bayes to imitate Dryden's mannerisms. "Like Dryden, Bayes prefers to dress in black and is fond of snuff and stewed prunes. His mistress, who takes the part of Amaryllis in the play that he is rehearsing, is an allusion to Dryden's mistress Anne Reeves, a pretty actress of small talent. Also, Bayes' appearance, his gestures, his dry and hesitant manner of delivery, as they were represented by John Lacy who originally played the role, were all modeled closely on Dryden's."[3]

[1] Allardyce Nicoll, *A History of English Drama 1660-1900* (Cambridge: University Press, 1961; first printing, 1923), Vol. 1, p. 248.
[2] George Villiers, Duke of Buckingham, *The Rehearsal*, ed. Montague Summers (Stratford-Upon-Avon: The Shakespeare Head Press, 1914), p. viii.
[3] Cedric Gale, ed., *The Rehearsal* and *The Critic* (Great Neck, N. Y.: Barron's Educational Series, 1960), p. 10.

Buckingham draws an exaggerated and artificial caricature in the figure of Bayes. The ridiculous traits are magnified and the clownish character of the poet is void of any redeeming characteristics that would render him human. Most of the time he remains on the stage and both his person and the play which he wrote, an absurd heroic drama, are the main targets of ridicule and laughter. Even the main design of *The Rehearsal* lends itself to the exploitation of the comic. Two men, Mr. Smith, who has recently arrived from the country, and Mr. Johnson, a sophisticated resident of the town, visit Bayes who is rehearsing his play in the theatre. Both visitors, fully aware of the follies of the author and the shortcomings of his play which is enacted in front of them, take every opportunity to point out the inadequacies of both. Thus laughter is evoked not only by the appearance and activities of Bayes and the performance of his play, but also by the comments of the two bystanders and the reaction of the actors who perform the play within the play.

Lacy's portrayal of Bayes-Dryden seems to have been a great success and it must have held a special appeal for the Restoration audience who recognized the original of the caricature. But, even without the allusions to and ridicule of a specific person Bayes remains a successful and entertaining comic character.

Bayes, the overenthusiastic author and director, sings, shouts, dances, fights, and dies along with his actors who perform his play. When he attempts to demonstrate how to fall down and play dead, he stumbles and hurts his nose. To cure the pain he wraps wet brown paper around the aching protrusion and continues to participate in his heroic drama. A frantic search for his eyeglasses ensues for he is not only shortsighted but also unable to decipher his own manuscript. Furthermore, his "peruke" falls off when he, in a moment of great puzzlement, scratches his head. Bayes' actions can hardly be called dignified and his mental state is suggested ironically in Prince Volscius' great "love and honor" speech.

The poet is so enamoured of the beauty of his own writing that he has to participate in the scene himself. The hero of the play, Prince Volscius, suddenly falls in love while he is pulling off his boots. He has to choose between love and honor and his dramatic hesitation is expressed in an elaborate metaphorical speech.

> Volscius.   My legs, the Emblem of my various thought
> Show to what sad distraction I am brought.
> Sometimes with stubborn Honour, like this Boot,

My mind is guarded, and resolv'd: to do't:
Sometimes, again, that very mind, by Love
Disarmed, like this other Leg does prove.
Shall I to Honour or to Love give way?
Go on, cries Honour; tender Love saies, nay!
Honour, aloud, commands, pluck both Boots on;
But softer Love does whisper put on none.
What shall I do? What conduct shall I find
To lead me through this twy-light of my mind?[4]

Not only Prince Volscius is vexed by not being able to make up his mind but so is Bayes whose grave problems constantly "puzzle his pate" (p. 47). He does not know yet how to end his play for his memory is so poor that he constantly forgets the names of his actors, and he has difficulties with logic. The opening scene of his drama is the so-called "whispering scene". Two characters, the physician and the gentleman-usher, whisper to each other and the audience hears only disjointed and unintelligible sentences. Smith asks for an explanation.

Smith. Well, Sir, but pray why all this whispering?
Bayes. Why, Sir, (besides that it is new, as I told you before) because they are suppos'd to be Politicians; and matters of State ought not to be divulg'd. (p. 17)

Although Bayes is unable at times to give logical explanations, he attempts to organize his thoughts and guide his life and activities by rules. He has three rules for writing, elaborate rules, which explain his practice of plagiarism. The first one is the rule of "Transversion or *Regula Duplex.* Changing Verse into Prose, or Prose into Verse, *alternative,* as you please" (p. 4). Bayes changes the writing of other authors by "transversing" or "transprosing" them until they are not traceable to the original source. The next rule is the "Rule of Record" (p. 4). The playwright visits a coffee house or "some other place where witty men resort" (p. 5). and jots down all clever remarks for use in his future plays. Smith wonders if Bayes has "no one Rule for invention" (p. 5). The writer takes out a little book from his pocket and reassures his visitor that he has a rule for this too: "Why, Sir, when I have anything to invent, I never trouble my head about it, as other men do; but presently turn over this Book, and there I have, at one view, all that Perseus, Montaigne, Seneca's Tragedies, Horace, Juvenal, Claudian, Pliny, Plutarch's lives and the rest, have ever thought upon the subject; and so,

---

[4] Villiers, *The Rehearsal*, p. 42. Further references to this play are given in text, by page-numbers only.

in a trice, by leaving out a few words, or putting in others of my own, the business is done" (p. 5).

Bayes also has rules for writing great prologues. One way of doing so is by "civility, by insinuation, good language, and all that", and the "other, by making use of some certain personal things, which may keep a hank upon such censuring persons, as cannot otherways, A gad, in nature, be hindered from being too free with their tongues" (p. 10). Bayes obviously favors the second rule.

Slander is not below the author's dignity and neither is revenge. The actors, eventually deciding that they have had enough of rehearsing the nonsensical play, quietly leave the theatre. When Bayes discovers that they are gone he swears: "I gad, I'l make 'em the most contemptible, despicable, inconsiderable persons, and all that, in the whole world for this trick. I gad I'l be reveng'd on 'em; I'l sell this play to the other House" (p. 71). The poet does not realize that his revenge is futile because nobody would wish to buy or act his play.

Though Bayes' temper occasionally gains the upper hand, he knows the rules of polite, proper, and refined behavior. His noble characters, the two kings of Brentford, lard their conversation with French words.

> 1. King.   You must being, *Mon foy.*
> 2. King.   Sweet, Sir, *Pardonnes moy.* (p. 19)

The author remarks after the conversation: "Bayes, Mark that : I makes 'em both speak French, to shew their breeding" (p. 20). Bayes himself shows his breeding by frequently, but not always properly, using French and Latin words. He woos the beautiful actress who plays the part of Amaryllis in his play by talking "bawdy" to her in French.

When it comes to making and understanding jokes, the poet seems to lack the necessary perception. Bayes thinks that he has a wonderful sense of humor but nobody laughs at his jokes. When he introduces the heroine, Amaryllis, he comments to Smith:

Bayes.   I'l tell you, now a pretty conceipt. What do you think I'l make 'em call her anon, in this Play?
Smith.   What, I pray?
Bayes.   Why, I make 'em call her Armarillis, because or her Armor; ha, ha, ha. (p. 7)

The author has also written a scene which, he assures Smith, "will make you dy with laughing if it be well Acted; for 'tis as full of Drollory as ever it can hold: 'tis like an Orange stuffed with Cloves, as for conceit" (pp. 29-30). The scene consits of dull and contrived "repartee" which amuses only Bayes. The poet is also amused by vulgarity and lets his characters "talk baudy; ha, ha, ha: beastly downright baudry upon the stage, I gad; ha, ha, ha; but with an infinite deal of wit, that I must say" (p. 43).

Bayes also finds it amusing that one of his heroic plays written in majestic and elevated style was not performed in the theatre.

Bayes. I gad, I can hardly tell you, for laughing (ha, ha, ha) it is so
        pleasant a story: ha, ha, ha.
Smith. What is it?
Bayes. I gad, the Players refus'd to act it. Ha, ha, ha.
Bayes. I gad they did it, Sir, point blank refus'd it; I gad, Ha, ha, ha.
        (p. 20)
Smith. That's impossible.

The poet takes insulting remarks for humor, fails to see the absurdity of really comic incidents and does not understand the ironical remarks made by the two observers.

Bayes the man is ridiculous enough, but Bayes the creative artist is even more so. Before he even sits down to write he goes through certain rituals which, together with rigid health rules, condition him for the right inspirational mood. When he intends to write poems he eats stewed prunes only, "but when I have a grand design in hand, I ever take Phisic, and let blood; for, when you would have pure swiftness of thought, and fiery flights of fancy, you must have a care of the pensive part. In fine, you must purge the Belly" (p. 18). He cautions Smith against taking snuff when he writes and explains to him, "Why, it spoil'd me once, I gad, one of the sparkishest Playes in all England. But a friend of mine, at Gresham Colledge, has promis'd to help me to some spirit of Brains, and I gad, that shall do my business" (p. 19).

Once Bayes is in the right mood he has no trouble producing master-works. After one of his songs is performed he exclaims, "Ha, Rogues! when I am merry, I write the things as fast as hops, I gad" (p. 33), and as for writing plays, "I can dispatch you a whole Play, before another man, I gad, can make an end of his Plot" (p. 36). He can compose and arrange forty dances in a day without much effort. The results of his creative efforts are disastrous and reflect clearly the incompetence ot their author.

Bayes even has difficulties explaining the plot of his drama to his visitors. He commences to unfold the intrigue but his story becomes unintelligible and muddled. The two visitors see most of the performance but the plot still does not seem to be clear to them. Johnson questions

Bayes and the author becomes upset and angry and blames his visitor.
When Smith complains that the story is disjointed, interrupted by ir-
relevant scenes and that the plot does not move, Bayes loses his temper.
" 'Plot stand still' why, what a Devil is the Plot good for, but to bring
in fine things?" (p. 31). The epilogue sums up Smith's and Johnson's
complaint:

> The play is at an end, but where's the Plot?
> That circumstance our Poet Bayes forgot. (p. 73)

Throughout the play the poet substitutes sensational and surprising
scenes and "devices" for a coherent story. He explains to his visitors:
"The grand design upon the stage is to keep the Auditors in suspense;
for to guess presently at the plot, and the sence, tires 'em before the end
of the first Act: now, here, every line surprises you, and brings in new
matter" (p. 6). The essential parts of the play are according to the
author the "Scenes, Cloaths and Dances" (p. 6). He wishes to please
the public and thus "you must ever interlard your Playes with Songs,
Ghosts and Dances" (p. 33).

Bayes loves that which is new and has only contempt for tradition and
authors of the past. He starts his play in a novel and startling way
because "I'll do nothing here that ever was done before, instead of
beginning with a Scene that discovers something of the Plot, I begin
this Play with a whisper" (p. 14). When Johnson wonders why Bayes'
imaginary country, Brentford, has two ruling kings, the author explains:
"Why? because it's new; and that's it I aim at. I despise your Johnson
and Beaumont, that borrow'd all they writ from Nature: I am for
fetching it purely out of my own fancy, I" (pp. 16-17).

The author has another new "device", an amazing contrivance
"for as every one makes you five Acts to one Play, what do me I, but
make five Playes to one Plot: by which means the Auditors have every
day a new thing" (p. 46). Equally surprising is the appearance of Lardel-
la who composed love poems when she was dying and now that her
soul has transmigrated into a "humble-bee" she hums them to her
lover and to the audience. Other novel entertainments include a grotesque dance depicting a moon eclipse, a coffin wheeled onto the stage
which opens up and "a Banquet is discover'd" (p. 51), and a scene
where Pallas Athena pours French wine from the shaft of her "conquer-
ing lance" and recites:

> . . . to appease your hunger, I
> Have, in my Helmet, brought a Pye:

> Lastly, to bear a part with these,
> Behold a Buckler made of Cheese. (p. 52)

The greatest surprise though is an altogether "new device" which Bayes describes with enthusiasm: "Why, Sir, I make a Male person to be in Love with a Female" (p. 46).

Bayes likes unusual scenes but his characters are mainly stock types. They appear on the stage without motivation as does Shirley who enters and says: "Hey ho, hey ho: what a change is here! Hey day, hey day! I know not what to do, nor what to say. (Exit)" (p. 26). Bayes discusses one character with his visitors, the great Drawncansir "a fierce Hero, that frights his Mistress, snubs up kings, baffles Armies, and does what he will, without regard to numbers, good manners, or justice" (p. 48). Smith wonders about the nature of a hero.

Smith. But, Mr. Bayes, I thought your Heroes had ever been men of great humanity and justice.

Bayes. Yes, they have been so; but for my part, I prefer that one quality of singly beating of whole Armies above all your moral virtues put together, I gad. (p. 48)

Drawncansir's main virtue though consists in drinking copiously. He snatches drinking cups from others and downs all the wine. When one character objects he makes a heroic speech:

> I drink, I huff, I strut, look big and stare;
> And all this I can do, because I dare. (p. 53)

Bayes' character portrayal is only surpassed by his poetry. He is inordinately proud of the language he uses and appreciates his own "delicate, dainty similes"' like his "allusion of Love" (p. 12).

> So Bear and Sow, when my storm is nigh,
> Snuff up, and smell it gath'ring in the sky;
> Boar beckons Sow to trot in Chestnut Groves,
> And there consummate their unfinish'd Loves:
> Pensive in mud they wallow all alone,
> And snore and gruntle to each others moan. (p. 13)

Bayes who loves figurative language finds a "general rule" for using it in poetry. He states "you must ever make a simile when you are surpris'd; 'tis the new way of writing" (p. 22). For his great heroic scene he advocates "forc'd conceipt, smooth Verse, and a Rant" (p. 54).

The difference between what Bayes thinks of himself and what the visitors believe him to be is great. The playwright is supremely self-confident. He believes himself to be an idealist and remarks to Johnson:

"I gad, I am not like other persons; they care not what becomes of their things, so they can but get mony for 'em; now, I gad, when I write, if it be not just as it should be in every circumstance, to every particular, I gad; I am no more able to endure it, I am not myself, I'm out of my wits, and all that, I'm the strangest person in the whole world. For what care I for mony? I write for Reputation" (p. 44). He visualizes himself as a great, but misunderstood writer: "This is the bane of all us Writers: let us soar but never so little above the common pitch, I gad, All's spoil'd; for the vulgar never understand it, they can never conceive you, Sir, the excellency of these things" (p. 31). He considers himself greater than Sir John Suckling and is convinced that his play is a master-work. He knows that its "design's good: that cannot be deny'd. And then, for language, I gad, I defie 'em all in nature to men it" (pp. 10-11). But, to make sure that the play will be a success he appoints "two or three dozen" (p. 11) of his friends to be ready in the pit on the day of the performance and if they clap "the rest you know must follow" (p. 11).

Smith and Johnson have less favorable opinions of Bayes and his activities. Smith, the outspoken country gentleman, voices his views most of the time in a straightforward and at times insulting manner whereas Johnson, the sophisticated *eiron*, comments in an ironical tone on the author's folly. Smith finds already the prologue "short indeed; but terrible" (p. 14), and as the play progresses, he finds it extremely foolish. Smith is bored when the play is not moving and remarks about Bayes' poetry: "Why there's no need for brain for this: 'tis but scaning, the labour's in the finger; but where's the sence of it" (p. 57). After Bayes explains one of his outlandish scenes to him Smith admits, "I confess Sir, you stupifie me" (p. 64). When Smith fails to understand another great scene he remarks to Johnson: "He is mighty ignorant, poor man; your friend here is very silly. Mr. Johnson, I gad, he is, ha, ha, ha" (p. 69).

When Bayes is absent from the stage Johnson can't conceal his con-tempt for him. He says to Smith, "I'l tell thee, Franck, thou shalt not see one Scene here worth one farthing", and remarks about the language, "when it comes to what he calls good language, it is, as I told thee, very fantastical, most abominably dull, and not one word to the pur-pose" (p. 17). But when Bayes is present Johnson ironically praises his endeavors and spurs him on to even greater folly. Bayes appreciates Johnson's praise and tells him, "A gad, you have a great deal of Wit" (p. 33). He explains how he came to this conclusion: "I know you have wit by the judgement you make of this Play; for that's the measure I go by: my Play is my Touchstone. When a man tells me such a one is a person of parts; is he so, say I? What do I do, but bring him presently to see this Play? If he likes it, I know what to think of him; if not, your most humble Servant, Sir, I'l no more of him upon my word, I thank you. I am a *Clara voyant*" (p. 33).

The two visitors have no desire to view the final battle scenes of Bayes' play and at an opportune moment they make their escape. When the author discovers their absence he rationalizes. He comes to the conclusion that his visitors are a "couple of senceless rascals, that had rather go to dinner than see this play out, with a pox to 'em. What comfort has a man to write for such dull rogues?" (p. 71).

Johnson finds Bayes entertaining but Smith, after observing the poet's antics for a while, remarks, "Pox on't but there's no Pleasure in him: he's too gross a fool to be laugh'd at" (p. 17). There are moments when this rather surly statement seems valid. The playwright is made up entirely of negative traits and unrelieved ignorance tends to be artificial and at times even tedious. Bayes's caricature resembles the exaggerated and stylized drawings of Jacques Callot of the seventeenth century and Claude Gillot of the early eighteenth century. Both artists depict *commedia dell' arte* characters with their fantastical costumes and grotesque poses.

Caricature though does not have to be artificial and gross to succeed. Sheridan's parody of bad plays and authors testifies that a gentler kind of satire can be most effective. Sheridan's play, *The Critic,* was written more than a century after Buckingham's satire. The subject is the same in both plays and so is the framework. The author is rehearsing his play and visitors comment on the action. What has changed considerably is the handling of character and caricature. Whereas Buckingham had one central figure, the ignorant Bayes, pitted against two men who are aware of his folly, Sheridan distributes the ridiculous traits among three fools, Dangle, "a mock maecenas to second-hand authors",[5] Sir Fretful Plagiary, a would-be author who has not the "slightest invention or original genius whatever" and is "the greatest traducer of all other authors living",[6] and Puff, the playwright and creator of *The Spanish Armada,* the tragedy performed on the stage, a "practitioner in panegyric" and a "professor in the art of puffing".[7] The visitors are much less "knowing" than Buckingham's observers. They have their own

5   Gale, *The Rehearsal* and *The Critic*, p. 120.
6   Gale, p. 126.
7   Gale, p. 134.

weaknesses and ridiculous traits which make them often the butt of laughter. The contrast between knowledge and ignorance is greatly reduced resulting in an intricate parody populated with gentle caricatures. Cedric Gale, who compares the two plays, writes about Sheridan's farce: "It has an air of geniality and a delight in foolishness that lessens its sting. Sheridan chuckles where Buckingham sneers."[8]

OUR CRAVING DAMOSELS: TYPE AND INDIVIDUAL

The lusty widow and the adulterous wife are not types invented by a Restoration dramatist. They existed in the ancient tales of India, the lively stories of *The Thousand and One Nights* and those relating the escapades of Greek deities. They appeared in the Latin comedies, the medieval fabliaux, and in Boccaccio's collection of tales, *The Decameron*. Chaucer's widow, the wife of Bath, reminds one that such characters existed in English literature before the seventeenth century.

However, Restoration drama was eminently suited to utilize this type on stage. The subject of comedy was usually the battle of the sexes and the butt of laughter, the loser, was the one who gave in before the battle started, whose strategy was easily recognized or who attacked without caution and decorum. Most likely there was another reason for the popularity of such characters at this time. The emancipation of women in the seventeenth century enabled them not only to participate in social life but they also invaded the theatre. Actresses played the female roles which had been previously performed by boys. Authors had a rich resource of talent to draw upon, such as Mrs. Knep who played Wycherly's Lady Fidget and My Lady Flippant, Mrs. Cory who performed the role of the Widow Blackacre, and the great Mrs. Leigh, who "ably personated . . . antiquated and odious specimens of old maidism or of wasted age",[9] and who acted Congreve's Lady Wishfort at the first performance of *The Way of the World*.

The figure of the wanton woman was familiar to the Restoration audience. In a type familiarity breeds laughter and the delight comes from recognizing certain traits and behavior in a character. If recognition is mixed with surprise then the author has usually transcended the type and created an individual. Most of the "craving damosels" of the Restoration theatre can be called types because they remain in the

---

[8]   Gale, p. 16.
[9]   Nicoll, *A History of English Drama 1660-1900*, p. 248.

boundaries of the expected and the familiar, but there are a few exceptions, a few characters who emerge as individuals and are worth remembering.

Thomas Shadwell created some of these types but he calls them humor characters. His definition of humor in the Preface to *The Humorists* is "the representation of some extravagance of Mankind".[10] The "extravagance" though is a familiar trait, and easily recognizable fault, because as he states, if such a humor would be shown on the stage "as only belongs to one, or two persons, it would not be understood by the Audience, but would be thought (for the singularity of it) wholly unnatural, and would be no jest to them neither".[11] Thus he endows his characters with typical traits. His Lady Cheatly is "The true Widdow, that comes to Town, and makes a show of a Fortune, to put off herself, and her two Daughters."[12] Another of his characters who will be included in the discussion as a type is Lady Loveyouth, "a vain amorous Lady, mad for a Husband, jealous of Theodosia, in love with Raymund."[13]

Among the traits which characterize the wanton women belongs dissimulation. The ladies feign to be what they are least: chaste, virtuous, and weary of men. Their pretentions are obvious to everyone except the most credulous fools. Among these often belongs the husband, as does Sir Paul Plyant, "an uxorious, foolish, old knight",[14] in Congreve's *Double Dealer*. Lady Plyant who is "very silly and thinks she has sense",[15] and who has an intrigue going on with Ned Careless, swears that her honor is "infallible and uncomeatable".[16] She is outraged though when it is suggested to her that the young Mellefont has designs upon her virtue. She and her husband confront Mellefont with indignation.

Lady Plyant. Have I behaved myself with all the decorum and nicety befitting the person of Sir Paul's wife? Have I preserved my honour as it were in a snow-house for these three years past? Have I been white and unsullied even by Sir Paul himself?

Sir Paul. Nay, she has been an invincible wife, even to me; that's the truth on't.

---

[10] Thomas Shadwell, *The Complete Works of Thomas Shadwell*, ed. Montague Summers (London: The Fortune Press, 1927), Vol. I, p. 186.

[11] *Ibid.*

[12] *Shadwell*, Vol. III, p. 287.

[13] *Shadwell*, Vol. I, p. 191.

[14] William Congreve, *Complete Plays*, ed. Alexander Charles Ewald (New York: Hill and Wang, 1964; first printing, 1956), p. 120.

[15] Congreve, p. 124.

[16] Congreve, p. 139.

Lady Plyant.   Have I, I say, preserved myself like a fair sheet of paper,
for you to make a blot upon?

The words virtue and honor are most often uttered by those women
who advocate conventional morality but do not practice it.

Frequently those who are most eager to get married and snare men
pretend to hate wedlock and the male sex. Horner, the connoisseur of
women, makes the following observation: "Women of quality are so
civil, you can hardly distinguish love from good breeding, and a Man
is often mistaken; but now I can be sure, she that shews an aversion to
me loves the sport, as those Women that are gone, whom I warrant to
be right: And then the next thing is your Woman of Honour, as you
call 'em, are only chary of their reputations, not their Persons, and 'tis
scandal they wou'd avoid, not Men."[17] Married women pretend to resist
the advances of men but give in with remarkable speed. Doralice in
Dryden's *Marriage a la Mode* swears: "Know, then, thou man of vain
imagination, know to thy utter confusion, that I am virtuous",[18] but in
the next moment she is willing to forget that she has a husband and
gives in to Palamede.

Sometimes the woman desires to catch a husband but often her aim is
only pleasure. Many are willing to go to extremes to achieve their goal
and their over-eagerness is only too obvious. In certain instances they
even visit notorious public places, like St. James' or the Exchange, to
pick up a man. Shadwell's Prologue to *The Humorists*, which is "written by a Gentlemen of Quality",[19] makes rather unflattering remarks
about women.

> Now for the Women –
> The little Fools into extreams are got,
> Either they are stone cold, or scalding hot.
> Some peevish and ill-bred, are kind to none;
> Others stark mad, in love with all the Town.
> The famous Eater had his Worm to feed,
> These Ramparts have a hungry Worm indeed.
> And as his ravenous Stomach made him get
> Tripes, Livers, and the coursest sort of Meat,
> Our craving Damosels, rather than stand out,
> Will any raw-bone Coxcomb run about.[20]

[17]   William Wycherly, *The Complete Plays*, ed. Gerald Weales (Garden City,
N. Y.: Doubleday, 1966), p. 263.
[18]   John Dryden, *The Works of John Dryden*, ed. John Loftis (Berkeley: University of California Press, 1966), Vol. VIII, p. 79.
[19]   Shadwell, *The Complete Works of Thomas Shadwell*, Vol. I, p. 190.
[20]   *Ibid.*

The widows seem to be especially hot and eager to corner their men. They dream about them: "Widows are mightily given to dream, insomuch that a dream is waggishly call'd the Widows Comfort."[21] Sir Frederick Frollick, in Etherege's *Love in a Tub*, remarks that "Widows must needs have furious flames; the bellows have been at work, and blown 'em up."[22]

In the battle of the sexes plotting and scheming are part of the game. The eager and designing women often have elaborate plans which most of the time are foiled either by their own folly or by the intervention of those who have no difficulty seeing through their efforts. In Restoration comedy there are many of these, not only Shadwell's gentleman of quality, but others, like Etherege's Dorimant who says, "I fathom all the depths of womankind",[23] or Congreve's Careless, who discusses with his friend the hot, amorous and scheming Lady Touchwood and comments: "Was there ever such fury! 'tis well Nature has not put it into her sex's power to ravish."[24] Thus not only the audience is aware of the frailties of the wanton women, but most of the time they are victimized by other characters in the play. Everyone seems to know their nature except themselves: they are often unaware of the thoughts of others and do not seem to realize that they are ridiculed by them. In many cases one questions if they have a real knowledge of morals.

Those who will be discussed as types are the Widow Bullfinch from Farquhar's *Love and a Bottle*, Lady Flippant, a widow from Wycherly's *Love in a Wood*, and the would-be widow, Lady Loveyouth, from Shadwell's play *The Humorists*. Among the married women Lady Cockwood of Etherege's *She Would If She Could* belongs to this group and also Wycherly's Lady Fidget from *A Country Wife*. Those who emerge as individuals are Congreve's old widow, Lady Wishfort, from *The Way of the World* and Widow Blackacre from Wycherly's *The Plain Dealer*.

Widow Bullfinch, who keeps a rooming-house and whose "dancing days are over",[25] does not belong to the upper classes as the rest of the characters do. She is fond of men and one of her lodgers is a poor poet who, as everyone knows, "pays his lodging by cracking some smutty Jests with his Landlady over-night; for she's well pleas'd with his natural

[21] Wycherly, *The Complete Plays*, p. 138.
[22] Sir George Etherege, *Plays and Poems*, ed. A. Wilson (London: John C. Nimmo, 1888), p. 26.
[23] Etherege, *Plays and Poems*, p. 314.
[24] Congreve, *Complete Plays*, p. 123.
[25] George Farquhar, *The Complete Works of George Farquhar* (New York: Godian Press, 1967; first printing, 1930), Vol. I, p. 29.

parts".[26] When a gentleman asks her to introduce him to the poet she hesitates: "I introduce you! no Widow dare be seen with a Poet, for fear she shou'd be thought to keep him."[27] The widow is lusty and demanding and the poet, Lyric, is tired and weary of the relationship. His "poor Pegasus is Jaded"[28] and he wants to free himself from slavery and the "Penance in a White Sheet".[29] His friend Pamphlet sympathizes with him: "Faith, I have often wonder'd how your Muse cou'd take such flights, yoak'd to such Cartload as she is."[30]

Equally typical though somewhat more complex is My Lady Flippant, "an affected Widow, in distress for a Husband, though still declaiming against marriage".[31] She has some money and a theory: "the Widows Fortune (whether suppos'd, or real) is her chiefest Bait, the more chary she seems of it, and the more she withdraws it, the more eagerly the busie gaping frye will bite; with us Widows Husbands are got like Bishopricks, by saying no" (p. 11). She tells others that she does not like or trust men, because, "Quacks in their Bills, and Poets in the titles of their Plays, do not more disappoint us, than Gallants with their promises" (p. 70). Indeed, she pretends to hate men and "whedle, jilt, trace, discover, countermine, undermine, and blow up the stinking fellows", and she is unaware when she utters the comic truth: "I never admitted a man to my conversation, but for his punishment certainly" (p. 42). When her friend Lydia reminds her that she was married and must have loved her husband at least, she says: "Fye, Madam do you think one so ill bred, as to love a Husband" (p. 68).

Lady Flippant though is eager to find a man at any cost. She haunts St. James Park at night and, when she finds only drunks one evening, she rails against the wine: "Oh drink, abominable drink; instead of inflaming Love, it quenches it, and for one Love it incourages, it makes a thousand impotent" (p. 33). When a man enters she is encouraged:

> But Fortune will not see me want, here comes a Bully,
> I whish he may stand;
> For now anights the jostling Nymph is bolder,
> Than modern Satyr with his Cloack o're shoulder. (p. 33)

Another evening she has even worse luck: "the Park affords not so

[26] Farquhar, p. 21.
[27] Farquhar, p. 30.
[28] Farquhar, p. 40.
[29] Farquhar, p. 41.
[30] *Ibid.*
[31] Wycherly, *The Complete Plays*, p. 9. Further references to Wycherly's *Love in a Wood* are given in text, by page-numbers only.

much as a Satyr for me, (an that's strange) no Burgundy man, or drunken Scourer will reel my way" (p. 96).

Once she has the opportunity to meet a man, her attack is bold and undisguised. She chases Dapperwit around the stage:

Flippant.   Dear, Mr. Dapperwit, merciful, Mr. Dapperwit.
Dapperwit.   Unmerciful, Lady Flippant.
Flippant.   Will you be satisfied?
Dapperwit.   Won't you be satisfied? (p. 69)

Dapperwit is saved when Lydia enters and he sighs: "Her Ladyship indeed, is the only thing in Petty-coats, I dread, 'twas well for me there was company in the Room; for I dare no more venture myself with her alone, than a Culley that has been bit, dares venture himself in a Tavern, with an old Rook" (p. 69).

Flippant's other victim is Sir Simon Addleplot. She is supposed to know him but she fails to recognize him because she is nearly blind. Lady Flippant is vain and confesses to one of her friends "my eyes are none of the best, since I have us'd the last new wash of Mercury water" (p. 76). When she encounters Addleplot sitting at a desk, writing, she thinks that he is a clerk. She "jogs" him energetically and she is irritated when Addleplot does not perceive what she wants. She says to herself: "There are some Clerks wou'd have understood me before this" (p. 74). She squeezes Addleplot to the wall, jogs him some more and after further efforts at last makes him understand her desires. The scene ends with the stage direction: "She throws down his Ink, and runs out, he follows her" (p. 75).

The situation is novel in Shadwell's *The Humorists* but Lady Loveyouth's character follows the expected pattern. Her husband Sir Richard left her after some "discontent". He found her vain, foolish, impertinent and forward,[32] left for Venice and later fought in a war. Lady Loveyouth has not heard of him for three years and presumes him to be dead. She pretends to be virtuous and even makes a "Vow of Widdowhood" (p. 203), which nobody believes. The young Raymund, who loves her niece Theodosia, voices his doubts about her vow: "I would as soon credit a Knight of the Post, as a protesting Widdow" (p. 209). Despite her statements that she will remain unwed and chaste, she not only allows two fools, Mr. Drybob and Mr. Briske, to make love to her (p. 202), but would like to lure Raymund away from her niece and marry him. She convinces herself eventually that "I am as unwilling to

[32] Shadwell, *The Complete Works of Thomas Shadwell*, Vol. I, p. 218. Further references to Shadwell's play are given in text, by page-numbers only.

marry as anybody; but you know where Marriages are made, alas,
there's no resisting our Fate" (p. 210). When her plans are foiled she is
willing to marry anyone, even the "diseas'd impotent fellow, that walking Hospital, Crazy" (p. 252), to "plague Raymund" (p. 240). She
would take any man, "for I am resolved to play at small game rather
than stand out" (p. 240).

Lady Loveyouth is perhaps more villainous than the other women
are. She is not only "ravenous" (p. 208) for men and an "impatient
Widdow" (p. 213), but intensely jealous and mean. She is pleased
when she receives news that her husband is dead and later, when she
learns that he is alive and that he stayed in her house disguised as a
servant, she can only show disappointment and concern for her own
welfare.

A much more entertaining and delightful figure is the Lady Cockwood
from Etherege's comedy *She Would If She Could*. The title of the play
clearly suggests Lady Cockwood's aspirations. She desires to have an
affair with the young and handsome Courtall who does everything to
escape her advances. He is rather cautious as "She is the very spirit
of impertinence, foolishly fond and troublesome, that no man above
sixteen is able to endure her" (p. 130). She would "give her lover no
more rest than a young squire that has newly set up a coach does his
only pair of horses" (p. 130).

To achieve her ends "madam Machiavel" (p. 207) schemes with
her maid Sentry, who helps her to think up "some lucky plot . . . to
get Sir Oliver out of the way" (p. 132). She states self-confidently: "I
am not a woman easily to be deceived" (p. 133), but Courtall manages
to escape from the "snares of the old devil" (p. 201) and outwit her.
The young man claims that "if her ladyship had got me into her clutches,
there had been no getting off without rescue" (p. 201). When his friend
suggests "thou shouldst fast thyself up to a stomach now and then, to
oblige her" (pp. 201-202), he objects: "I know not what I might do in
a camp, where there was no other woman; but I shall hardly in this
town, where there is such plenty, forbear good meat, to get myself an
appetite to horseflesh" (p. 202).

One moment the Lady Cockwood pretends to be virtuous; the next
she is ready to make an assignation and tells the reluctant Courtall:
"Me thinks you are too scrupulous, heroic, Sir" (p. 164). She constantly
assures her husband of her conjugal fidelity, her devotion to him and
convinces him of her "scrupulous tenderness to her honour" (p. 184).

Lady Cockwood differs though from the previous characters and seems closer to being an individual than either Lady Flippant or Lady Loveyouth. She is not only a major character who is worked out in greater detail than the previous figures were but she is capable of using psychology at times. She is aware of her husband's foibles and is able to maneuver him in a rather amusing way. Sir Oliver gets periodically drunk, misbehaves, insults his wife, and then is chastised by his spouse and does penance. Lady Cockwood exploits this behavior to its fullest; and when Courtall reports that her husband is on one of his binges, she tells him: "If Sir Oliver be in that indecent condition you speak of, to-morrow he will be very submissive, as it is meet for so great a misdemeanour; then can I feigning a desperate discontent, take my own freedom without the least suspicion" (p. 148). Another rather individualistic trait in her is her tendency to accuse others of her own shortcomings. Lady Cockwood accuses the two young girls who stay in her house of being careless with their reputation and virtue: "I could wish Sir Joslin would remove 'em, for fear they should bring an unjust imputation on my own honor" (p. 150). She also accuses Courtall whom she tried to seduce of making a "foul attempt" upon her honor (p. 193).

Etherege's Lady Cockwood is somewhat out of the ordinary and so is Wycherly's Lady Fidget whose portrait is drawn in bold strokes. She is crude but she is also honest and dynamic. Lady Fidget is a "pretender to honour"[33] but she is perfectly aware that she is dissimulating, unlike the other types who become entangled in their own lies and believe in their deception. "Our Reputation, lord! Why should you not think, that we women make use of our Reputation, as you men of yours, only to deceive the world with less suspicion; our virtue is like the Stateman's Religion, the Quakers Word, the Gamesters Oath, and the Great Man's Honour, but to cheat those that trust us" (p. 351). She pretends to be shocked when her husband uses the expression "naked truth" in his conversation, "Fy, Sir Jasper, do not use that word naked" (p. 285); but, when she is in a company where she feels free, she becomes rather uninhibited and even obscene. After she consumes two bottles of wine she is willing to "unmask" herself and speak the "truth". She admits that she dislikes her husband and complains that "women of quality, like richest stuffs, lye untumbled, and unasked for" (p. 350).

The Lady Fidget's concept of honor is fashioned to suit her own ap-

---

[33] Wycherly, *The Complete Plays*, p. 285. Further references to Wycherly's *A Country Wife* are given in text, by page-numbers only.

petites. As long as she is not found out, everything is permissible and honorable: "a Woman of honour looses no honour with a private Person" (p. 284). A man of honor is one who is capable of satisfying her desires and who does not destroy her reputation. She likes her men young, wild, and forward: "We take freedom from a young person as a sign of breeding, and a person may be as free as he pleases with us, as frolick, as gamesome, as wild as he will" (p. 351).

The brutal honesty of Lady Fidget lends a novel touch to the character of the wanton woman. Lady Fidget has more awareness than either the Widow Bullfinch or Lady Loveyouth. Like Lady Cockwood, she knows her husband and in her relation with him is the victimizer rather than the victim. The cuckold seems to be even less aware than the wife who in turn is usually victimized by her lover or other "knowing" characters in the play. Despite her greater awareness Lady Fidget somehow still remains inside the limitations of a type and never becomes an individual.

On the other hand, vanity is the only trait which inhibits the Widow Blackacre, another one of Wycherly's comic personages. She is outraged when somebody suggests that she is older than she actually is, or pretends to be. Otherwise Wycherly reverses the pattern which one usually expects to find in the character of the husband-hunting, lusty widow. The Widow Blackacre does not as "other country ladies do ... come up (to town) to be fine, cuckold their Husbands and take their pleasure".[34] She is perfectly aware what people expect from a typical widow and she is outraged that she is mistaken for such one: "You think with us Widows, 'tis no more than up, and ride. Gad Forgive me, now adayes, every idle, young, hectoring, roaring Companion, with a pair of turn'd red Breeches, and a broad Back, thinks to carry away any Widow, of the best degree" (p. 433). Widows, particularly those who have money, are very special people, although everyone thinks that marrying a Widow is an "easie business, like leaping the Hedge, where another has gone over before; a Widow is a mere gap, a gap with them" (p. 506). Wycherly reminds one of the widow-pattern and thus points the ironic contrast in the Widow Blackacre's behavior.

Unlike the other ladies she does not pursue men but is chased by two of them, Oldfox and Freeman. Both are rather fond of her fortune and the young and handsome Freeman is especially adamant in his pursuit. He promises all those pleasures the usual widow-type would welcome.

---

[34] Wycherly, *The Complete Plays*, p. 401. Further references to Wycherly's *The Plain Dealer* are given in text, by page-numbers.

He argues: "... you have no business anights Widow; and I'll make you pleasanter business than any you have; for anights I assure you, I am a man of great business" (p. 432). He even promises to be "impudent and baudy" (p. 285). The Widow Blackacre is reluctant because she prefers the "business" of dabbling in the law to the "business" Freeman promises.

She is a would-be lawyer who not only enjoys being involved in countless law-suits but also speaks the legal jargon of the profession. She is as "vexatious as her Father was, the great Attorney" (p. 401), and is a "litigious She-Pettyfogger, who is at Law and difference with all the World" (p. 285). As long as she stays single she can pursue her hobby because she is responsible for her own affairs and has the legal right to engage in law-suits. Matrimony, on the other hand, would deprive her of the "benefit of the Law", and that would be "worse than Excommunication" (p. 504).

The Widow Blackacre is nearly blackmailed into marriage by Freeman who discovers some of the indiscretions she has committed in the past. The Widow avoids matrimony by drawing up a rather unusual agreement which would benefit both her and the young man, who lacks money: "I am contented you should hold and enjoy my person by Lease or Patent; but not by the spiritual Patent, call'd Licence; that is to have the priviledges of a Husband without the dominion; that is *Durante beneplacitio*: in consideration of which, I will out of my jointure, secure you an Annuity of Three hundred pounds a Year, and pay your debts" (p. 508).

Typical lusty widows are usually not accompanied by their strapping, teenage children. But Blackacre keeps a constant eye on her Jerry, takes him along wherever she goes and rules him with an iron hand. Jerry is at an age when he is eager to read adventure stories, like *The Seven Champions of England,* eat candy, and even visit occasionally the quarters where the maids live. His mother though, who wishes to make a lawyer of him, buys him law books, orders him to memorize endless, boring law cases and denies him an allowance. After a miniature rebellion, Jerry, with the help of Freeman, blackmails his mother. The Widow Blackacre has to give in and promise her son forty pounds a year as an allowance, a horse, and free "ingress, egress, and regress to and from" the maids' garret (p. 509). Thus not only Blackacre's all consuming hobby but also the little family drama contribute to the shaping of an individual.

The Widow is subdued and outwitted thanks to her own past mistakes and not because she is deceived by the nature of others. She knows that Oldfox is a "debauch'd, drunken, leud, hectoring, gaming Companion" who wants "some widow's old Gold to nick upon" (p. 436), and though her opinion of Freeman is somewhat harsh there is truth in her statement: "I say, you are a worn-out Whoremaster at five and twenty in Body and Fortune" (p. 285), and "you wou'd have me keep you . . . that you might turn keeper" (p. 285).

As Blackacre's past indiscretions are revealed, it is evident she suspects people of the worst because her own activities at times have been rather questionable. In her salad days the widow seems to have had a gay time. She is familiar with the private rooms of the Cock in Bow Street and assures two gentlemen who wish to keep their visit to the inn secret: "You are safe enough, Gentlemen, for I have been private in this house ere now, upon other occasions, when I was something younger" (p. 505). It is not only revealed that Jerry was born "before Wedlock" (p. 508) but also that the widow paid "two Knights of the Post" to forge four deeds, three wills and counterfeit "Hands and Seals to some six Bonds" (p. 505).

To create an individual, Wycherly utilizes first of all the atypical and to heighten its impact he contrasts it with the typical. He carefully works out details such as the widow's speech-pattern, and enlarges the scope of the character by including events from her past. She belongs to the category of characters who are partially aware and most of the time she is the target of laughter not because she is familiar, but because she is surprising and unique.

It is more difficult to render a satisfactory explanation of Congreve's method of painting an individual. Lady Wishfort of his *The Way of the World* retains many of the typical traits of the love-starved widow yet she transcends the type and manages to become a most remarkable individual.

In *The Way of the World*, we actually have two widows, Mrs. Wishfort and her daughter, Arabella, who was once married to Mr. Languish. Soon after her husband's death Arabella had an affair with the engaging Mirabell and when she became pregnant by him, she married Mr. Fainall. As a widow she did what a typical widow is supposed to do but as a married woman she is faithful to her husband. Her mother is "full of the vigour of fifty-five",[35] she "will breed no more" (p. 298), and is an "antidote to desire" (p. 354). The footman who saw her

---

[35]   Congreve, *Complete Plays*, p. 298. Further references to Congreve's *The Way of the World* are given in text, by page-numbers.

once early in the morning before she put on her makeup has some doubts that he saw her ladyship: "Why, truly, sir, I cannot safely swear to her face in the morning, before she is dressed, 'Tis like I may give a shrewd guess at her by this time!" (p. 298). In daytime when she is prepared to meet people she does not dare to frown "because her face is none of her own, S'heart, an she should, her forehead would wrinkle like the coat of a creamcheese" (p. 365).

Both Lady Wishfort and Widow Blackacre are conscious of the public image of a wanton widow. They try to avoid conforming to that image and Blackacre succeeds by acting unlike a typical widow. Despite her awareness and her attempts not to fall into the pattern Lady Wishfort fails and ironically does exactly what she endeavors to avoid.

The witty Mirabell is aware that "the good lady would marry anything that resembles a man, though 'twere no more than what a butler could pinch out of a napkin" (p. 317). When Waitwell, the butler who is disguised as Sir Rowland, is ordered to court Lady Wishfort, the widow yields quickly and is willing to marry him the same day. However she tries to justify her speedy surrender: "you must not attribute my yielding to any sinister appetite, or indigestion of widowhood; nor impute my complacency to any lethargy of continence" (pp. 353-354). She feels reassured when Waitwell tells her that she is "all camphor and frankincense, all chastity and odour" (p. 354).

Mirabell had also courted her, flattered her and played on her vanity because he wished to be near her lovely niece, Millamant.

I did as much as man could, with any reasonable conscience; I proceeded to the very last act of flattery with her, and was guilty of a song in her commendation. Nay, I got a friend to put her into a lampoon, and compliment her with the imputation of an affair with a young fellow, which I carried so far, that, I told her the malicious town took notice that she was grown fat of a sudden; and when she lay in a dropsy, persuaded her she was reported to be in labour. The devil's in't, if an old woman is to be flattered further, unless a man should endeavour downright personally to debauch her; and that my virtue forbade me. (pp. 289-299)

Lady Wishfort falls in love with Mirabell and even thinks that he'll marry her, but when she finds out that he dissembled, her adoration turns into passionate hatred. Like Lady Loveyouth, she is willing to marry any man to avenge herself. Yet, when he later asks for forgiveness, she softens and even admits to herself: "Oh, He has witchcraft, in his eyes and tongue! When I did not see him I could have bribed a villain to his assassination; but his appearance rakes the embers which have so long lain smothered in my breast" (p. 366). Mrs. Fainall, her daughter, and Mirabell understand her foolish involvements only too well:

> Mrs. Fainall.   Female frailty! we must all come to it, if we live to be old, and feel craving of a false appetite when the true is decayed.
>
> Mirabell.   An old woman's appetite is depraved like that of a girl – 'tis green sickness of a second childhood; and, like the faint offer of a latter spring, serves but to usher in the fall, and withers in an affected bloom.

Lady Wishfort, like Lady Flippant, pretends to hate men and when she educates her daughter she tries "to impress upon her tender years a young odium and aversion to the very sight of men" (p. 361). Lady Wishfort is also incredibly vain. Her morning toilet is one of the great comic scenes of the play and when she hears that Mirabell presumably called her "superannuated" she is ready to have "him poisoned in his wine" (p. 326). She also likes her liquor as Lady Flippant did but, whereas Wycherly's craving damosel boldly admits that she is tippling, Lady Wishfort hides the bottle when she hears somebody coming. She is intensely aware of decorum and attempts to act in the proper way whenever it is possible.

The ironical blend of ignorance and knowledge is not only present when Lady Wishfort behaves like a typical widow but also in those acts and traits which help to make her a unique being. She is certainly not uneducated. The books she keeps in her room and offers as "entertainment" to one of her visitors are rather proper: "Quarles and Prynne, and 'The Short View of the State' with Bunyan's works" (p. 325). Her knowledge of various literary works is revealed through her rich and colorful comparisons. When her maid, Peg, does not hide the bottle quickly enough under the table she grumbles: "This wench has lived in an inn upon the road, before she came to me, like Maritornes the Austrian in Don Quixote!" (p. 324). When in the final act all the characters meet she remarks about two of them: "Here come two more of my Egyptian plagues" (p. 364). And when Mirabell is announced she protests: "I fear I cannot fortify myself to support his appearance. He is terrible to me as a gorgon; if I see him I fear I shall turn to stone, and petrify incessantly" (p. 298).

The original comparisons and also the highly imaginative language Lady Wishfort uses help to establish the uniqueness of her personality.

When she is angry at Mirabell she hopes to reduce him to "frippery and rags! a tatterdemalion! I hope to see him hung with tatters, like a long-lane pent-house or a gibbet thief. A slander-mouthed railer! I warrant the spendthrift prodigal's in debt as much as the million lottery, or the whole court upon a birthday" (p. 326). When Lady Wishfort discovers her maid's treachery she reminds her that she saved her "from washing of old gauze and weaving of dead hair, with a bleak blue nose over a chafing-dish of starved embers, and dining behind a traverse rag, in a shop no bigger than a birdcage!" (p. 356).

Lady Wishfort is sometimes perfectly aware of the nature of those around her and other times she is entirely blind. She knows that Sir Wilful would not make a suitable husband for her niece: "It will never make a match — at least before he has been abroad" (p. 352). She is aware that her son-in-law is a "barbarian" (p. 363), but she fails to recognize the evil nature of Mrs. Marwood and the disguise of the butler-suitor, Sir Rowland.

The same is true of her perception of her own nature. She can look into the mirror, admit that she looks old and "errantly flayed — I look like an old peeled wall" (p. 327). She believes though that throughout her life she had been an example of virtue for her daughter (p. 360). When in the end of the play, Mrs. Fainall is proven virtuous and wise, she exclaims "O daughter, daughter! 'tis plain thou hast inherited thy mother's prudence!" (p. 370).

The emotional depth of a type is usually limited. The love-starved widow desires and lusts but does not love; she is brimming with anger, fustration, and vengeance, but she does not know insight and forgiveness. Lady Wishfort is angry at Sir Rowland and Mirabell, whom she hates "worse than a quaker hates a parrot, or than a fishmonger hates a hard frost" (p. 308), and against whom she swears vengence in the most colorful terms. But eventually she is able to forgive both of them. She also deeply loves her daughter and would do anything for her, give up her fortune, and even the right to marry again.

Lady Wishfort is also a romantic. She is ridiculously flustered when she prepares to meet Sir Rowland for the first time and tries out different poses and attitudes which would be becoming to her: "Tenderness becomes me best — a sort of dyingness ... a swimmingness in the eye" (p. 327). When she is disappointed she is ready to "retire to deserts and solitudes, and feed harmless sheep by groves and purling streams" (pp. 359-360).

In the last scene of the play, it is revealed that Mrs. Fainall, during the time she was a widow, cautiously and prudently provided for her future. She made her love, Mirabell, the guardian of her estate before she married her second husband. When Fainall is ready to abscond with his wife's fortune and finds out that he has no access to it he is reminded by Mirabell: " 't is the Way of the World, Sir, of the widows of the world" (p. 369). It is evident from this statement that Congreve utilizes the type and the ways of the widows. But after examination of Mrs. Wishfort it is also obvious that Congreve's character surpasses that which is typical and expected.

The individual has not only a more complex personality than the type but also has traits which are all his own and do not fit the pattern. A type can be entirely unaware, but this is certainly not true for the unique personality. It is also evident from the comparison of Blackacre and Wishfort that not only the atypical makes an individual but sometimes the type can be evolved into an uncommon and orginal personage. Congreve's Lady Wishfort, as do the characters of Johnson and Molière, bears witness that singularity can be achieved even with the use of a pattern.

A SILLY-WISE ROGUE: THE PARTIALLY AWARE CHARACTER

In the Preface to *The Humorists* Shadwell makes the following observations about character portrayal: "Good men, and men of sence, can never be represented but to their advantage, nor can the Characters of Fools, Knaves, Whores, or Cowards (who are the people I deal most with in Comedies) concern any that are eminently so".[36] He feels that "good men, and men of sence enough may have blind-sides ... may have errors, but they are not known by them, but their excellencies".[37] Shadwell believes that these men can be represented on the stage and that they do not have to be perfect. Congreve's "sententious" Mirabell loves Millamant with all her frailties:

I like her with all her faults; nay, like her for her faults. Her follies are so natural, or so artful, that they become her; and those affectations which in another woman would be odious, serve but to make her more agreeable. I'll tell thee, Fainall, she once used me with that insolence, that in revenge I took her to pieces; sifted her, and separated her failings; I studied 'em, and got 'em by rote. The catalogue was so large, that I was not without

[36]   Shadwell, *The Complete Works of Thomas Shadwell*, Vol. I, pp. 185-186.
[37]   Shadwell, p. 186.

hopes one day or other to hate her heartily: to which end I so used myself to think of 'em, that at length, contrary to my design and expectation, they gave me every hour less and less disturbance; till in a few days it became habitual to me to remember 'em without being displeased. They are now grown as familiar to me as my own frailties; and in all probability, in a little time longer, I shall like 'em as well. [38]

Not only are "men of sence" often more appealing when their wisdom is mixed with folly but dunces seem to be also more human if their stupidity is tempered by some comprehension and insight. Etherege's Sir Fopling Flutter is not a complete booby. His entrance is preceded by a discussion of fools. Medley, Emilia, and Lady Townley comment on the issue:

Medley.	Fools will make you laugh.
Emilia.	For once or twice, but the repetition of their folly after a visit or two grows tedious and unsufferable.
Lady Townley.	You are a little too delicate Emilia.
Page.	Sir Fopling Flutter, Madam, desires to know if you are to be seen.
Lady Townley.	Here's the freshest fool in town and one who has not cloyed you yet. [39]

After he leaves the room on another occasion he is again discussed by those who enjoyed his company:

Medley.	A fine mettled coxcomb.
Dorimant.	Brisk and insipid.
Medley.	Pert and dull.
Emilia.	However you despise him, gentlemen, I'll lay my life, he passes for a wit with many. [40]

Sir Fopling is accepted by some because he is young, quite good looking, he behaves well and, according to the clever Harriet, "Varnished over with good breeding many a blockhead makes a tolerable show."[41] Etherege's Sir Fopling Flutter is somewhat less of a fool than the dunce of his *Love in a Tub,* Sir Nicholas Culley. But, Etherege does not deal with the complexities of human nature and his charming, witty comedies are not geared to exploit the vagaries of semi-wits and semi-fools.

Wycherly and Congreve, on the other hand, from the very beginning of their careers aim to portray persons who are made up of a mixture

---

[33] Congreve, *Complete Plays*, p. 301.
[39] Etherege, *Plays and Poems*, pp. 294-295.
[40] Etherege, p. 299.
[41] Etherege, p. 283.

of ignorance and knowledge. In his first play, *Love in a Wood*, Wycherly indicates his interest in various degrees and kinds of folly. Dapperwit holds a long discourse on classes of wits. "There are as many degrees of Wits, as of Lawyers; as there is first your Sollicitor, then your Aturney, then your Pleading-Counsel, then your Chamber-Counsel, and then your Judge; so there is first your Court-Wit, your Coffee-Wit, your Poll-Wit or Pollitick-Wit, your Chamber-Wit or Scribble-Wit, and last of all, your Judge-Wit or Critick."[42]

In the same play Wycherly also illustrates the difference between a fool and a semi-fool, the culley and the would-be wit. Sir Simon Addleplot is upset when he is told that he is taken for Dapperwit's "Culley". "I his Culley? . . . Lord that I should be thought a Culley to any Wit breathing."[43] Mrs. Joyner, who discusses this matter with him, counsels him: "Nay do not take it so to heart, for the best Wits of the Town are but Culleys themselves."[44] This does not seem to console Addleplot and he decides: "I will throw off Dapperwits acquaintance when I am marryed, and will only be a Culley to my wife, and that's no more than the wisest Husband of 'em all is."[45] Dapperwit himself is outwitted and ridiculed throughout the play. He is one of the many "Witwouds" of Restoration comedy, halfway between the blockheads and the true-wits.

"A silly-wise Rogue wou'd make one laugh more than a stark Fool", remarks Sparkish, the would-be-wit of Wycherly's *The Country Wife*.[46] In this play Wycherly has gained complete mastery of depicting characters and especially portraying those who are partially aware. His ability is acquired to a great extent from Molière and one is reminded of Arnolphe from *The School For Wives* when one takes a closer look at Pinchwife.

Like Arnolphe, Pinchwife is keenly aware of the ways of the town and the ways of the wits who like to cuckold husbands. The forty-nine-year-old Pinchwife, who has recently married a young and pretty country girl, takes all the precautionary measures against being deceived but is unable to escape from being fooled. He tells Horner, the true-wit of the play, who eventually succeeds in cuckolding him: ". . . my Wife shall make me no Cuckold, though she had your help Mr. Horner; I understand the Town, Sir" (p. 270). He knows the town-tricks, the

---

[42] Wycherly, *The Complete Plays*, p. 37.
[43] Wycherly, p. 17.
[44] Wycherly, p. 37.
[45] *Ibid.*
[46] Wycherly, *The Complete Plays*, p. 279. Further references to Wycherly's *The Country Wife* are given in text, by page-numbers.

town-wits, and the "naughty Town Women, who only hate their Husbands, and love every Man else, love Plays, Visits, fine Coaches, fine Cloaths, Fidles, Balls, Treates, and so lead a wicked Townlife" (p. 275).

Pinchwife also knows everything about adultery, mainly because before he married he was a "Whoremaster, one that knew the Town so much, and Women so well" (p. 269). Now that he is married he is obsessed with the supposition that he himself might become a cuckold. When he sees men walking on the street he identifies them as a "swarm of Cuckolds and Cuckold-makers" (p. 269). When he looks at the signs hung outside the inns and sees "the Bull's head, the Rams-head, and the Stags-head", he comments that they are "every husbands proper sign" (p. 300). Sparkish, his future brother-in-law does not relieve his anxiety when he reminds him "we men of wit have amongst us a saying, that Cuckolding like the small Pox comes with a fear, and you may keep your Wife as much as you will out of Danger of infection, but if her constitution incline her to't, she'l have it sooner or later by the world, say they" (p. 338).

Pinchwife is so afraid of being cuckolded that he becomes as jealous as "a Cheapside Husband of a Covent-garden Wife" (p. 272). His excessive distrust drives him to take ridiculous precautionary measures. He tries to conceal from everyone that he is married and when he is found out, he tries to convince the wits that his wife is ugly and stupid. He is eventually caught in his own lies and gives them up when he finds his match in three prying and curious ladies: "Well, here is no being too hard for Women at their own weapon, lying, therefore I'l quit the Field" (p. 283). Whenever it is possible he locks his wife in her room and once when he takes her out to town he tries to disguise her by dressing her up in boy's cloaths.

Pinchwife knows the nature of those around him. He is perfectly aware that Horner is clever and that he intends to seduce his wife. He is also much more perceptive than Sparkish, the would-be-wit, who intends to marry Pinchwife's sister, Alithea. Sparkish introduces his friend Harcourt to his future wife. Harcourt falls in love with her and confesses his passion for her in front of the bridegroom, who does not at all comprehend what is going on. Pinchwife is present and has no trouble sizing up the situation. He tries to warn Sparkish and tells him that he is blind. When the young man does not believe him he gets angry: "How, Sir, if you are not concern'd for the honour of your Wife, I am for that of a Sister; he shall not debauch her: be a Pander to your own Wife, bring Men to her, let 'em make love before your face, thrust 'em into a corner together, then leav'em in private! is this your Town wit and conduct?" (p. 279).

Although Pinchwife recognizes the deception of others he is blind to his wife's ways and without knowing it he has become her "culley". Unaware that he is deceived, he carries her love letter to Horner and eventually even leads her to him. Sparkish, the fool, does not recognize his rival disguised as a priest. Similarly Pinchwife fails to recognize his wife dressed in Alithea's clothes. In both cases Wycherly indicates the two men's inability to see beyond the surface, the mask that covers the true nature of man.

At times Pinchwife has sound ideas and knows what he should or shouldn't do. Other times he seems to have lost his judgment and reason. He makes the mistake of telling his wife all about the evil diversions and pleasures of the town, forbidding her to indulge in them. Alithea is aware that instead of discouraging the young wife "he is setting her a-gog upon them himself" (p. 275). When Pinchwife goes so far as to tell his wife that "one of the lewdest Fellows in town" who saw her in the theatre "told me he was in love with you" (p. 276), even he realizes that he made a mistake and admits, "I've gone too far, and slipt before I was aware; how overjoy'd she is" (p. 276)). Later, when his wife praises Horner, he thinks to himself: "So 'tis plain she loves him, yet she has not love enough to make her conceal it from me, but the sight of him will increase her aversion for me, and love for him" (p. 318).

Pinchwife's inflexible way of thinking is shown by his love for maxims. Like Molière's Arnolphe he has a set of rules for a successful marriage: "Good Wives, and private Soldiers shou'd be ignorant", and therefore, "I'll keep her from instructions, I warrant you" (p. 269). Another of Pinchwife's proverbial wisdoms states: " 'tis my maxime, he's a Fool that marrys, but he's a greater that does not marry a Fool" (p. 270). Women for him are all the daughters of Eve; "out of natures hands they came plain, open, silly and fit for slaves" (p. 319), but love makes "these dow-bak'd, sensless, indocile animals, Women, too hard for us Politick Lords and Rulers" (p. 337).

Pinchwife, the "Politick Lord" or according to his wife a "musty husband" (p. 360), is much more lifelike than Sparkish the typical would-be-wit and bubble. But he has no deep emotions as Arnolphe does, who discovers that he is betrayed and also that he deeply and sincerely loved the woman who left him for another. Arnolphe is never as vicious and unpleasant as his English counterpart, who pinches his wife, and threatens her with sword and knife. Pinchwife knows other people; he knows the way of men, though at times his set views make him unable to be flexible enough to deal with problems he encounters. He does not possess any depth of feeling or understanding and does not show any signs of humility and self-realization.

Wycherly involves his audience with the character by making him human and alive but he does not let the viewer sympathize or really identify with him. The shrewd, unpleasant, ridiculous Pinchwife remains the butt of contemptuous laughter, not removed from life by his artificiality as Sparkish is, but not loved or accepted either.

In his "Commendatory Verses to my dear Friend Mr. Congreve, on his Comedy Called 'The Double-Dealer' ", Dryden identifies the strength of his contemporary authors. He praises Etherege for his "courtship" and "manly Wycherly" for his "satire, wit and strength", and Congreve he commends for the sweetness of his manner.[47] Wycherly's silly-wise Rogues are bitter fools who evoke censure and contemptuous laughter. Congreve's mixed characters are usually delightful people who elicit as a response sympathy and benevolent amusement. He achieves this response by frequently endowing his fools with a touch of self-knowledge, the ability to catch a glimpse of their own folly and admit it in a delightful and goodnatured way. Sometimes Congreve allows his characters to gain insight and develop, and other times he reveals their humanity by suggesting their hidden problems, their pathetic everyday struggle with the ravages of old age, with lack of self-confidence or loneliness.

In Congreve's first play, *The Old Bachelor,* even the greatest fools attain a degree of insight. Congreve's cuckold-candidate is called Fondle-wife who, unlike Pinchwife who orders people around and punishes them if they do not obey, intends to reason with his wife "Cocky". He tells his servant Barnaby:

Go and bid my Cocky come out to me. I will give her some instructions, I will reason with her, before I go. (Exit Barnaby) And, in the meantime, I will reason with myself. – Tell me, Isaac, why art thee jealous? Why art thee distrustful of the wife of thy bosom? – because she is young and vigorous, and I am old and impotent. Then, why didst thee marry, Isaac? – because she was beautiful and tempting, and because I was obstinate and doting, so that my inclination was, and is still greater than my power. And will not that which tempted thee, also tempt others, who will tempt her, Isaac? – I fear it much.[48]

---

[47] Congreve, *Complete Plays,* p. 114.
[48] Congreve, *Complete Plays,* p. 77.

The two boobies of the play are Sir Joseph Wittol and his body-guard, Captain Bluffe, a *miles gloriosus* type. It is not beyond Sir Joseph to admit: "Well, I am a fool sometimes — but I am sorry."[49] He blindly believes in Bluffe's bravery and his tall tales of heroic endeavors, but, when he sees his companion beaten and humiliated, he finds out the truth about him. He does not get angry but in a very gentle and tactful way tries to console him: "no matter, 'tis past. . . . Come, we'll think no more of what's past."[50] Another time Sir Joseph and Bluffe overhear a conversation conducted by two crooks, Setter and Sharper:

Sharper.	Impossible! Araminta take a liking to a fool!
Setter.	Her head runs on nothing else, nor she can talk of nothing else.
Sharper.	I know she commended him all the while we were in the Park; but I thought it had been only to make Vainlove jealous.
Sir Joseph.	How's this? (Aside to Bluffe) Good bully, hold your breath, and let's hearken. Egad, this must be I.
Sharper.	Death, it can't be! – an oaf, an idiot, a wittol!
Sir Joseph.	(Aside) Ay, now it's out: 'tis I, my own individual person.
Sharper.	A wretch, that has flown for shelter to the lowest shrub of mankind, and seeks protection from a blasted coward.
Sir Joseph.	(Aside) That's you, bully back.[51]

Sir Joseph Wittol admits freely that he is a blockhead, but Sir Sampson Legend, of Congreve's *Love for Love,* has to be taught a lesson before he acquires humility enough to admit that he is an old fool.

Sir Joseph is not at all as ignorant as his old friend Foresight who is "an illiterate old fellow, peevish and positive, superstitious, and pretending to understand Astrology, Palmistry, Physiognomy, Omens, Dreams, etc."[52] Sir Sampson enjoys imitating Foresight's pseudo-scientific language, cracks jokes at his expense, and loves to tell him tall tales. "I know the length of the Emperor of China's foot; have kissed the Great Mogul's slipper, and rid a hunting upon an elephant with the Cham of Tartary — Body o' me, I have made a cuckold of a king, and the present majesty of Bantam is the issue of these loins" (p. 220).

Sir Sampson proves himself an old fool in his dealing with two young people, his son Valentine and the clever and beautiful Angelica, whom Valentine desires to marry. Sir Sampson objects to his son's spend-

---

[49]   Congreve, p. 58.
[50]   Congreve, p. 72.
[51]   Congreve, pp. 99-100.
[52]   Congreve, *Complete Plays*, p. 198. Further references to Congreve's *Love for Love* are given in text, by page-numbers.

thrift ways, intends to disinherit him and leave his estate to his younger son, Ben. He not only fails to recognize his son is virtuous, in love, and ready to mend his ways, but he also maliciously visualizes his punishment after he is left without a penny: "Odd, I love to see a young spendthrift forced to cling to an old woman for support, like ivy round a dead oak: faith I do; I love to see 'em hug and cotton together, like down upon a thistle" (p. 237). When Valentine pretends to be insane so that he won't be forced to sign the document which will disinherit him, Sir Sampson pretends to be a concerned and loving father and tries to cajole his son into signing his name. Valentine's friend is amazed at the sudden show of fatherly warmth and remarks: "Miracle! the monster grows loving!" (p. 256). Valentine, who knows his father, is not fooled by his histrionics and says after Sir Sampson leaves: "That grey hairs should cover a green head, and I make a fool of my father" (p. 257).

Sir Sampson grows loving also when he encounters Angelica, who pretends that she is willing to marry him. He is pleased: "Faith and troth, you're a wise woman" (p. 237), and his language grows flowery as he courts her, just as Sir Epicure Mammon's does when he woos Doll Common in Jonson's *The Alchemist*.

> come forth,
> And taste the air of palaces; eat, drink
> The toils of emp'rics, and their boasted practice;
> Tincture of pearl, and coral, gold, and amber;
> Be seen at feasts and triumphs; have it ask'd,
> What miracle she is; set all the eyes
> Of court a-fire, like a burning glass,
> And work 'em into cinders, when the jewels
> Of twenty states adorn thee, and the light
> Strikes out the stars.[53]

Sir Sampson courts Angelica with: "If I had Peru in one hand, and Mexico in t'other, and the eastern empire under my feet, it would make me only a more glorious victim to be offered at the shrine of your beauty" (p. 272; Sir Epicure's Speech). He assures her that he is not a "bare courtier" (p. 270) at the age of fifty, and tells Angelica " 'twere pity you should be thrown away upon any of these young idle rogues about the town. Odd, there's ne'er a young fellow worth hanging!" (p. 271). When Angelica consents to marry him he becomes flustered and emotional: "Odzooks I'm a young man: odzooks, I'm a young man, and I'll make it

[53] *English Drama 1580-1642*, ed. C. F. Tucker Brooke and N. B. Paradise (Boston: C. D. Heath and Co., 1933).

appear. Odd, you're devilish handsome: faith and troth, you're very handsome; and I'm very young, and very lusty. Odsbud, hussy, you know how to choose, and so do I; — odd, let me kiss it; 'tis warm and as soft — as what? — Odd, as t'other hand; give me t'other hand, and I'll mumble 'em and kiss 'em till they melt in my mouth" (p. 273).

Sir Sampson finds out that Angelica has tricked him only to be able to marry Valentine. "I always loved your son and hated your unforgiving nature. I was resolved to try him to the utmost; and I have tried you too, and know you both. You have nor more faults than he has virtues; and 'tis hardly more pleasure to me, that I can make him and myself happy, than that I can punish you" (p. 283). Sir Sampson Legend at last realizes his mistakes and turns to Foresight: "You're one illiterate old fool and I am another" (p. 284).

In the same play one encounters Tattle, who pretends to be a "keeper of secrets" (p. 208), but is in reality an outrageous scandal-monger. He refuses to divulge the names of ladies with whom he is supposed to have had affairs, but he makes sure by his detailed descriptions of the women that everybody will recognize them. He is a name-dropper, a snob, and is even uneducated. Jeremy, the perfect butler, who was educated in Cambridge tells Tattle:

Jeremy.   . . . I'm as secret as the head of Nilus.
Tattle.   Ay! who is he, though? a privy counsellor?
Jeremy.   (Aside) O ignorance! – (Aloud) A cunning Egyptian, sir, that
           with his arms would over-run the country: yet nobody could
           ever find out his headquarters.
Tattle.   Close dog! a good whoremaster, I warrant him.

What gives humanity and complexity to Tattle is the suggested discrepancy between what Tattle is, what he pretends to be and what he would like to be. Tattle pretends to be discreet, one who wouldn't divulge anything even faintly questionable. Angelica tries to get him to speak about his exploits and baits him:

Angelica.   . . . For certainly Mr. Tattle was never never denied anything
             in his life.
Tattle.   O Lord! yes, indeed madam, several times.
Angelica.   I swear I don't think 'tis possible.
Tattle.   Yes, I vow and swear I have: Lord, madam, I'm the most
             unfortunate man in the world, and the most cruelly used by
             the ladies. (p. 233)

Tattle pretends, but one has the feeling that the tragi-comic truth is revealed in his statements. This is also evident when he is accused of bragging with his conquests, and he assures the company:

Tattle.	. . . I have been the most unsuccessful creature living, in things of that nature; and never had the good fortune to be trusted once with a lady's secret, not once.
Angelica.	No!
Val.	Not once, I dare answer for him.
Scan.	And I'll answer for him; for I'm sure if he had, he would have told me. – I find, madam, you don't know Mr. Tattle. (pp. 233-234)

Tattle's mock-humility ends quickly when his ability to conquer is seriously questioned by the company and he is ready to prove to everyone that he is successful, beloved and sought after.

Tattle.	. . . I can show letters, lockets, pictures, and rings; and if there be occasion for witnesses, I can summon the maids at the chocolate-houses, all the porters at Pall-Mall and Covent-Garden, the door-keepers at the play-house, the drawers at Locket's, Pontac's, the Rummer, Spring-Garden; my own landlady, and valet-de-chambre; all who shall make oath, that I receive more letters than the Secretary's Office; and that I have more Vizor-masks to inquire for me than ever went to see the Hermaphrodite, or the Naked Prince. (p. 235)

Tattle wants to be a Don Juan, boasts that he was called "Turk-Tattle", and assures his friends, "I was the famous Tattle, who had ruined so many women" (p. 235).

Is Tattle refused by women or do they flock to him? Why does he have to boast and indulge in what Angelica calls an "insolent piece of vanity" (p. 235). One gets also a glimpse of reality, Tattle's real exploits. He is certainly not without charm and is able to seduce Prue who has lived in the country and is only too eager to learn the city-ways from Tattle. Eventually the gullible Tattle is tricked into marrying Mrs. Frail for whom he has never had any "thoughts of serious kindness". At least he does not think only about his misfortune but also feels sorry for Mrs. Frail: "I never liked anybody less in my life. Poor woman! Gad, I'm sorry for her, too; for I have no reason to hate her neither; but I believe I shall lead her a damned sort of life" (p. 281).

Although Tattle is exceedingly amusing, there is a touch of Chaplinesque pathos about him. His clown-mask seems to slip at times and one catches a fleeting glimpse of the man beneath it. The same is true of Petulant, one of the silly-wise rogues of Congreve's *The Way of the World*. When one considers Petulant, though, it is impossible to forget about his constant companion and best friend Anthony Witwoud. Both of them attend the Lady Wishfort's cabal nights and pay court to the lovely Millamant. Squire Witwoud is discussed and characterized by the true wits Mirabell and Fainall, who are aware of his virtues and shortcomings.

Fainall.   ... he has something of good-nature and does not always want wit.

Mirabell.   Not always: but as often as his memory fails him, and his common-place of comparisons. He is a fool with a good memory, and some few scraps of other folks' wit. He is one whose conversation can never be approved, yet it is now and then to be endured. [54]

Witwoud and Petulant presumably are the best friends and agree "like treble and bass" but when occasionally Petulant feels like contradicting or gets drunk, they indulge in "raillery" and "namecalling" (p. 333). The insight into the secret life of Petulant is provided by Witwoud, who in his friend's absence is ready to reveal his faults. He divulges to Mirabell and Fainall that Petulant "has a smattering-faith and troth, a pretty deal of an odd sort of a small wit", but he has "no more breeding than a bum-bailiff" and "in a controversy, he'll contradict anybody" (p. 304). After a long row of such remarks Witwoud states: "I can defend most of his faults, except one or two: one he has, that's the truth on't; if he were my brother, I could not acquit him" (p. 304). After long hesitation and further disparaging of his friend Witwoud admits Petulant's major and unforgivable fault; "He will lie like a chambermaid, or a woman of quality's porter" (p. 305).

As an answer to the last remark a coachman appears at the door and asks for Petulant: "Three gentlewomen in a coach would speak with him" (p. 305). Witwoud enlightens the company that "these are trulls whom he allows coach-hire, and something more, by the week, to call on him once a-day at public places" (p. 305). Although it seems that nobody cares to see Petulant, he has no visitors and does not receive any letters, he is eager to be thought popular and beloved. Thus he hires callers and, according to Witwoud, "this is nothing to what he used to do; — before he found out this way, I have know him call for himself" (p. 305). When Fainall wonders what this means Witwoud is ready to give an explanation: "Mean! why he would slip you out of this chocolate-house, just when you had been talking to him — as soon your back was turned — whip he was gone! — then trip to his lodging, clap on a hood and scarf, and a mask, slap into a hackney-coach,

[54] Congreve, *Complete Plays*, p. 302. Further references to Congreve's *The Way of the World* are given in text, by page-numbers.

and drive hither to the door again in a trice, where he would send in for himself; that I mean, call for himself, wait for himself; nay, and what's more, not finding himself, sometimes leaves a letter for himself" (pp. 305-306). Witwoud predicts that Petulant will not go to the door "because there's no more company here to take notice of him" (p. 305). Petulant is called, he comes, refuses to go out to see the ladies and tells the company "let 'em snivel and cry their hearts out" (p. 306). He nonchalantly tells his friends that two "co-heiresses" are waiting for him outside and dismisses Betty the maid who tells him "they are gone, sir, in great anger", with "Enough, let them trundle. Anger helps complexion, saves paint" (p. 272).

At Petulant's amusement Witwoud is made most uncomfortable when his past is revealed by a visiting half-brother. It seems before Witwoud became a fop and town-wit, he was an "attorney's clerk" and lived with "honest Pimple Nose the Attorney of Furnival's Inn" (p. 336). Witwoud is certainly distinguishable by his malice, his pseudo-wit and his pretentions, but Petulant's loneliness, his desire to be noticed and his bizarre solution make him not easy to forget.

It seems that the most usual way to lift out a character from the rank of unadulterated fools is by giving him insight into another person. Levels of ignorance are thus easily established and occasional identification with a character is made possible. We laugh with Sir Sampson at Foresight and we even watch with Pinchwife the bubbling of Sparkish. This kind of brief camaraderie does not necessarily establish any close sympathy, and the audience is ready to turn against the character the moment he becomes the butt of laughter. Sir Fopling's breeding is pleasant, though neither knowledge of manners nor a smattering of intelligence does much to lift a character out of the group of dunces. Sir Sampson's imagination delights and so does Lady Wishfort's knowledge of Don Quixote and Greek mythology, but such knowledge is decidedly less appreciated than wisdom. To wisdom belongs self-knowledge, a glimpse and acknowledgement of one's frailties, and an awareness of deeper feelings: love, tenderness, forgiveness, and compassion. The silly-wise fools who have gained this knowledge belong to the world of the living — the men of all times.

III

FIELDS OF IGNORANCE AND KNOWLEDGE (I)

MIRTH IN THE COMPANY OF FOOLS:
HUMOR AND LEVELS OF INTELLIGENCE

> 'Tis not so hard to counterfeit joy in the depth of
> affliction, as to dissemble mirth in a company of fools.[1]

"What a man discerns to be ludicrous reveals the extent of his intelligence, his wit, and his culture", remarks Schilling in *The Comic Spirit*.[2] Each age and culture has its own brand of humor and this is particularly discernible in seventeenth century France and England. The polished, self-conscious wit of the sparkling courts of Louis XIV and Charles the Second is not only cultivated in the salons of high society but also incorporated in the comedies of the age. Playwrights learn from the courtiers and imitate the chiseled maxims of Francois de Marsillac, duc de la Rochefoucauld, and the insolent, but delightful, poems and aphorisms of Charles Sedley, Charles Sackville, the Earl of Dorset, and those of John Wilmot, the Earl of Rochester.

The clever and "knowing" characters of the stage show their mental agility by incorporating maxims and finely wrought similes into their repartee whereas the fools use inept puns, tell clumsy jokes, or vainly struggle to create an acceptable simile. The wits are by no means kind and their merriment is often achieved at the expense of others. Among comic characters one also finds those partially aware ones who make fun of the dunces who are less intelligent than themselves, but who in their turn are ridiculed by more accomplished "raillers".

Most Restoration playwrights are successful in creating a hierarchy of dunces whose intelligence is defined by the humor they produce and

---

[1] William Congreve, *The Double Dealer* in *Complete Plays*, ed. Alexander Charles Ewald (New York: Hill and Wang, 1964; first printing, 1965), p. 157.
[2] Bernard N. Schilling, *The Comic Spirit: Boccaccio to Thomas Mann* (Detroit: Wayne University Press, 1965), p. 17.

enjoy. Shadwell realizes that this is not an easy task and he compliments his mentor, Ben Jonson, by commenting on his ability to "put wit into the mouth of the meanest of his people, and which, is infinitely difficult, made it proper for 'em".[3]

It seems to be a universal attitude that those who are least intelligent express their merriment with physical action. Mockmode, from *Love and a Bottle*, makes the discovery that "Wit lies in Jingling".[4] and consequently he breaks all the glasses at the inn. He remarks: "I have often heard there was Wit in breaking Glasses. It would be a very good Joke to break the Flask now."[5] Wycherly's Novel defines humor as "Railing, Roaring, and making a noise".[6] He also derives merriment from "Cutting Napkins and Hangings".[7] Oldfox, his drinking-companion, disapproves of his activites and tells him: "There's Mischief, if you will; but no Wit, or Humor."[8]

One step above the "wits" who like to break glasses and make noises are those who are fond of telling bad jokes and who wonder why their humor is not appreciated. Wycherly's Dapperwit, after attempting to entertain his companions, is told that he is forcing "chaw'd jests" and "mouldy Lampoones" on his listeners.[9] Dapperwit is convinced that he has a remarkable sense of humor as is Sir Samuel Hearty; "A brisk, amorous, adventurous, unfortunate Coxcomb; one that by help of humorous, nonsensical By-Words, takes himself to be a Wit".[10] Farquhar's Clincher Junior who had been reared in the country has a rather curious sense of humor. He appears in town dressed in fancy clothes and explains his sudden affluence:

Lady Darling.	Bless me Cousin! how came ye by these cloaths?
Clincher.	Cloath! Ha, ha, ha, the rarest Jest! Ha, ha, ha, I shall burst, by Jupiter Ammon, I shall burst.
Darling.	What's the Matter, Cousin?

[3] Thomas Shadwell, *The Complete Works of Thomas Shadwell*, ed. Montague Summers (London: The Fortune Press, 1927), Vol. I, Preface to *The Humorists*, pp. 188-189.
[4] George Farquhar, *Love and a Bottle* in *The Complete Works of George Farquhar* (New York: Gordian Press, 1967; first printing, 1939), Vol. I, p. 31.
[5] Farquhar, pp. 31-32.
[6] William Wycherly, *The Plain Dealer* in *The Complete Plays*, ed. and intro. Gerald Weales (Garden City, N. Y.: Doubleday, 1966), p. 500.
[7] Wycherly, p. 501.
[8] *Ibid.*
[9] Wycherly, *Love in a Wood* in *The Complete Plays*, p. 18.
[10] Shadwell, *The Virtuoso* in *The Complete Works of Thomas Shadwell*, Vol. III, p. 104.

Clincher.	The Matter! Ha, ha, ha: Why an honest Porter, ha, ha, ha, has knock'd out my brother's Brains, ha, ha, ha.
Wildair.	A very good Jest, i'faith, ha, ha, ha.
Clincher.	Ay Sir, but the best Jest of all is, he knock'd out his Brains with a Hammer, and so he is as dead as a Door-nail, ha, ha, ha.
Darling.	And do you laugh, Wretch?
Clincher.	Laugh! ha, ha, ha, Let me see e're a younger Brother in England that won't laugh at such a Jest. [11]

Ben's "sea-wit" in Congreve's *Love for Love* is certainly an improvement over Clincher's morbid country-wit, but is still censored by those who have to listen to it. Ben, according to Sir Sampson, is "a very wag! only a little rough, he wants a little polishing."[12] Mrs. Frail, who because she believes that Ben will inherit a fortune wants to marry him, pretends to appreciate his jokes, at least until he compares her to a "tight vessel" and tells her:

Ben.	Marry, and I should like such a handsome gentlewoman for a bedfellow hugely; how say you, mistress, would you like going to sea? Mess, you're a tight vessel! and well rigged, an you were but as well manned.
Mrs. Frail.	I should not doubt that, if you were master of me.
Ben.	But I'll tell you one thing, an you come in a high wind, or that lady – you mayn't carry so much sail o' your head. – Top and top-gallant, by the mess.
Mrs. Frail.	No, why so?
Ben.	Why, an you do, you may run the risk to be overset, and then you'll carry your keels above water, he! he! he!

Petulant, another of Congreve's comic characters having a sense of humor, causes his friends some anxiety when he is in a joking mood and states: "I am in humour to be severe."[13]

| Mirabell. | Are you? pray then walk by yourselve: let not us be accessory to your putting the ladies out of countenance with your senseless ribaldry, which you roar out aloud as often as they pass by you; and when you think you have made a handsome woman blush, then you think you have been severe. [14] |

Petulant's friends avoid his company when he is "severe". Others greet a bad joke often with a frozen silence and the only one who laughs

[11] Farquhar, *The Constant Couple* in *The Complete Works of George Farquhar*, Vol. I, p. 147.
[12] Congreve, *Love for Love* in *Complete Plays*, p. 239.
[13] Congreve, *The Way of the World* in *Complete Plays*, p. 309.
[14] *Ibid.*

is the fool who tells it. Manly, one of Wycherly's characters, calls those who will laugh at their own jests "Bartholomew-Fair Buffoons", [15] as the performers at the fair were crude and their jokes lacked subtlety and wit. At times even these are perceptive enough to notice that nobody else laughs at their jokes. When Sparkish entertains his friends, Horner, Harcourt, and Dorilant, with elaborate and contrived witticisms, the wits become impatient and are ready to stop him. Horner is the only one who is willing to give him another chance.

Horner.   . . . hear him out; let him tune his crowd a while.
Harcourt.   The worst Musick the greatest preparation.
Sparkish.   Nay faith, I'll make you laugh. . .[16]

He continues his narrative and after delivering the punchline roars with laughter. He does not perceive that he is the only one who is amused and proceeds to tell about the fabulous reception his story received at another gathering.

Sparkish.   With that they all fell a laughing, till they bepiss'd themselves; what, but it do's not move you, methinks? well see one had as good go to Law without a witness, as break a jest without a laughter on ones side. [17]

Shadwell's Drybob who is pleased with his excellent sense of humor and without modesty tells his friend: "I am amaz'd to think how the Thoughts come into my Head. I am, as to matters of Jests, as my Friend Ovid was in Verses."[18] Drybob has a simple explanation for people's not laughing at his jokes. He remarks about his friend Brisk, who listens without a smile to his witticisms: "He, pshaw! a pox on him, he has not wit; a damn'd dull fellow, he cannot break a jest in an hour."[19] Thus Drybob labels Brisk a dullard and continues to enjoy his own jokes.

The dunces who have little or no sense of humor have trouble not only telling jokes but also understanding them. They laugh at the wrong times and find hilarious that which is not at all funny. Shadwell's foolish poet, Ninny, is ready to be amused at any statement; and when he bursts out laughing at a perfectly straight statement, he explains to the baffled speaker: "ha, ha, ha, — Now have you said the Best thing

[15] Wycherly, *The Plain Dealer*, p. 426.
[16] Wycherly, *The Country Wife* in *The Complete Plays*, p. 267.
[17] *Ibid.*
[18] Shadwell, *The Humorists*, Vol. I, p. 205.
[19] *Ibid.*

in the World, and do not know it."[20]   Congreve's Sir Joseph Wittol has
the tendency to discover humor in his own speeches and appreciatively
roars after one of his remarks: "Ha, ha! ha! a very good jest I profess,
ha! ha! ha! a very good jest, and I did not know that I had said it, and
that's a better jest than t'other."[21] One of Wycherly's clever women,
Hippolita, is aware that her not too bright fiance, Monsieur, has very
little sense of humor, but prides himself on understanding and appreciat-
ing jokes. She exploits his vanity, proposing a "jest". Hippolita sends
Monsieur to his rival, the man she actually loves and desires to marry,
with a message that she wishes to elope with him. Monsieur is highly
amused at such a wonderful joke and promises to make his rival "look
so sillily".[22] He delivers the message, loses his bride and discovers that
the jest wasn't very good after all.

A very frequently portrayed comic character in Restoration Comedy
is the man who mistakes an insult for a joke. He interprets rudely told
remarks aimed at humiliating him as "raillery" or a jest, to which
he should respond with laughter. Wycherly makes frequent use of this
kind of character. Sparkish, the would-be-wit from *The Country Wife*,
responds to Harcourt's insults by saying: ". . . if he does rail at me,
'tis but in jest I warrant; what we wits do for one another and never
take any notice of it".[23] Congreve's Tattle is also highly amused when he
is told by Scandal, "thou never hadst to do with anybody that did not
stink to all the town."[24] Shadwell's Ninny is delighted when he is told by
the surly Stanford: "I had rather be at a Bear-Garden then be in your
Company",[25] and by the outspoken Emilia: "You are a most abominable
fool, and the worst Poet in Christendom".[26]

Sometimes playwrights combine several of these traits just discussed
creating from them a comic character whose ignorance manifests itself
predominantly by his lack of humor. Two such personages are Congreve's Lord Froth and Dryden's Bibber.

William Bibber, the tailor, is inordinately fond of jokes and thanks
to this weakness he becomes everybody's dupe. Failer, a gallant, who
would like to dress well but has no money to pay for his clothes, is

[20] Shadwell, *The Sullen Lovers* in *The Complete Works of Thomas Shadwell*.
Vol. I, p. 25.
[21] Congreve, *The Old Bachelor* in *Complete Plays*, p. 55.
[22] Wycherly, *The Gentleman Dancing-Master* in *The Complete Plays*, p. 136.
[23] Wycherly, *The Country Wife*, p. 280.
[24] Congreve, *Love for Love*, p. 208.
[25] Shadwell, *The Sullen Lovers*, p. 42.
[26] *The Sullen Lovers*, p. 43.

advised by his friend, Burr, to seek out Bibber and entertain him with good stories. "Break but a Jest, and he'll beg to trust thee for a Suit; nay, he will contribute to his own destruction."[27] Burr feels uneasy, "I ne'r made Jest in all my life",[28] but Failer assures him that "A bare clinch will serve the turne; a Carwhichet, a Quaterquibble, or a Punn."[29] Failer exploits the tailor and so does Loveby who lodges with the Bibbers. He does not pay his rent, seduces Mrs. Bibber, and openly mocks and insults her husband. Bibber is delighted and amused: "There was wit now; he called me Cuckold to my face."[30] The tailor though wants his rent-money, but when Loveby threatens that he'll pay but "from henceforward I'l keep my wit for refin'd spirits",[31] Bibber changes his mind and lets him stay without payment.

Isabell, a visitor to the tailor's shop, tries to warn him about Mrs. Bibber's activities and says: "Look to your Wife, Sir, or in time she may undo your trader, she'll get all men-Customers to her self."[32] Bibber is enchanted at such a wonderful joke, falls on his knees before her and begins to take her measurements. When Isabell wonders at his behavior, he hurriedly explains: "I must beg your ladiship e'n to have the honour to trust you but for your Gown, for the sake of that last jeast. Flowr'd Satten, wrought Tabby, Silver upon any grounds; I shall run mad if I may not trust your Ladiship."[33]

Congreve's Lord Froth is a more intricately drawn character than the mad tailor, Bibber. He is a "solemn Coxcomb",[34] a fool who takes himself seriously and feels insulted when his friend Sir Plyant imbibes champagne and calls him a merry man.

Lord Froth.	O foy, Sir Paul! what do jou mean? Merry! O barbarous! I'd as lieve you called me a fool.
Sir Paul.	Nay, I protest and vow now, 'tis true; when Mr. Brisk jokes, your lordship's laugh does so become you, he! he! he!
Lord Froth.	Ridiculous! Sir Paul, you're strangely mistaken, I find champagne is powerful. I assure you, Sir Paul, I laugh at nobody's jests but my own or a lady's; I assure you, Sir Paul.

[27] John Dryden, *The Wild Gallant* in *The Works of John Dryden*, eds. John Harrington Smith and Dougald MacMillan (Berkeley and Los Angeles: University of California Press, 1962), Vol. III, p. 9.
[28] *Ibid.*
[29] *Ibid.*
[30] *The Wild Gallant*, pp. 13-14.
[31] *The Wild Gallant*, p. 16.
[32] *The Wild Gallant*, p. 50.
[33] *Ibid.*
[34] Congreve, *The Double Dealer*, p. 120.

Brisk.	How? how, my lord? what, affront my wit! let me perish, do I never say anything worthy to be laughed at?
Lord Froth.	O foy! don't misapprehend me, I don't say so, for I often smile at your conceptions. But there is nothing more unbecoming a man of quality than to laugh; 'tis such vulgar expression of the passion! everybody can laugh. Then, especially to laugh at the jest of an inferior person, or when anybody else of the same quality does not laugh with one; ridiculous! To be pleased with what pleases the crowd! Now when I laugh, I laugh always alone.
Brisk.	I suppose that's because you laugh at your own jests, egad, ha! ha! ha!
Lord Froth.	He! he! I swear, though, your raillery provokes me to a smile.
Brisk.	Ay, my lord, 'tis a sign I hit you in the teeth if you show 'em. [35]

Because Lord Froth is unable to discern between what is serious and what is funny he always makes the wrong choice, laughs at the wrong time at the wrong jokes and remains serious when everyone else is amused. His theory, in a way, makes sense because it is safest for him to laugh at his own jests. Even when he goes to the theatre he avoids laughing, and when he is asked why he bothers to see a comedy he explains: "To distinguish myself from the commonalty, and mortify the poets: the fellows grow so conceited when any of their foolish wit prevails upon the side-boxes, — I swear — he! he! he! I have often constrained my inclination to laugh, — he! he! he! to avoid giving them encouragement."[36] The only occasion when the solemn Sir Froth feels safely amused is at a gathering when the members of the company maliciously gossip about those who are absent and laugh at the expense of their acquaintances.

Those who can neither tell nor perceive a joke are the dunces of comedy. On a somewhat higher level one finds the unsuccessful simile-makers. The witty characters in Restoration comedy frequently use and also appreciate clever comparisons. Congreve's Oxford-educated butler, Jeremiah, entertains his master Valentine with perfectly turned similes and Millamant remarks to her lover "Sententious Mirabell — Prithee don't look with that violent and inflexible wise face like Solomon at the dividing of the child in an old tapestry hanging."[37] Wycherly's Harcourt and Dorilant attempt to define the nature of a mistress. Ac-

---

[35] *The Double Dealer*, pp. 125-126.
[36] *The Double Dealer*, p. 126.
[37] Congreve, *The Way of the World*, p. 321.

cording to Harcourt, "Mistresses are like Books; if you pore upon them too much, they doze you, and make you unfit for Company; but if us'd discreetly, you are the fitter for conversation by 'em." On the other hand Dorilant feels that, "A Mistress shou'd be like a little Country retreat near the Town, not to dwell in constantly, but only for a night and away; to taste the Town better when a Man returns."[38] Shadwell's Belfond Junior upsets Termagant, his former mistress, by telling her that "Mistresses, like green pease, at first coming, are only had by the Rich, but afterwards they come to everybody."[39]

When the would-be-wits attempt to dazzle their audience with witty comparisons, their lack of imagination and good sense becomes evident to all. In Wycherly's *The Country Wife*, even Lucy, the maid, feels only contempt toward Sparkish, who often uses silly comparisons. She remarks about him: "He has been a great bubble by his similes as they say."[40] Sparkish accuses Alithea, his fiancee, of being unfaithful to him. She is an "unworthy false woman, false as a friend that lends a man mony to lose, false as dice, who undoe those that trust all they have to 'em".[41] Congreve's Witwoud only misinterprets jokes and "so passionately affects the reputation of understanding raillery, that he will construe an affront into a jest",[42] but he is also censured for his "common-place" comparisons.[43] Whereas Sparkish employs wrong and inappropriate comparisons, Witwoud's limitation is his use of trite and unimaginative similes. He receives a letter from his brother and remarks that it is "as heavy as a panegyric in a funeral sermon, or a copy of commendatory verses from one poet to another".[44] According to Witwoud "friendship without freedom is as dull as love without enjoyment or wine without toasting".[45] He remarks to his companion, Petulant: "Thou are an epitomiser of words. ... Thou art a retailer of phrases; and dost deat in remenants of remenants, like a maker of pin-cushions — thou art in truth (metaphorically speaking) a speaker of shorthand."[46]

Sparkish and Witwoud belong to the hierarchy of semi-fools as often do those who engage in "raillery". The word itself seems to refer to a

[38] Wycherly, *The Country Wife*, p. 264.
[39] Shadwell, *The Squire of Alsatia* in *The Complete Works of Thomas Shadwell*, Vol. IV, p. 227.
[40] *The Squire of Alsatia*, p. 346.
[41] *Ibid.*
[42] Congreve, *The Way of the World*, p. 302.
[43] *Ibid.*
[44] *The Way of the World*, p. 303.
[45] *The Way of the World*, p. 305.
[46] *The Way of the World*, p. 349.

number of activities. It sometimes means simply a witty exchange of
words and at other times merely describes bantering and teasing. Raillery also frequently connotes amusement at the folly of other people and
exposure of their shortcomings and mistakes. In all these activities
there is often to be found a touch of cruelty and malice. A seventeenth-
century writer has a rather ambiguous view of merriment at the expense
of other people. Sometimes he extolls those who engage in it, but at
other times takes a critical view of those who are unkind and sets them
up as targets of ridicule. This ambiguous attitude is noticeable in
Molière's plays. Célimène's witty mockery of members of the court is
applauded, whereas Arnolphe is censured for the same behavior. He
laughs at all the husbands of the town who have been cuckolded, only
to be warned by Chrysalde that he should not gloat at their misfortune.

> mais qui rit d'autrui
> Doit craindre qu'en revanche on rie aussi de lui.[47]

Arnolphe becomes the butt of laughter by the end of the play and is
punished for his lack of sensitivity and understanding.

The same ambiguous attitude is discernible in Restoration comedy.
"I love to be malicious", says Brisk. "Nay, deuce take me, there's
wit in't too."[48] Congreve's pretty Belinda delights to walk in the park
and "laugh at the vulgar; both the great vulgar and the small".[49]
Wycherly's Freeman also likes to amuse himself at the expense of
fools, remarking to his friend Manly, "the pleasure which Fops afford
is like that of Drinking, only good when 'tis shar'd; and a Fool, like
a bottle, which makes you merry in company will make you dull alone".[50]
There seems to be implied criticism of Freeman's attitude. The speaker
is gay and witty but he is also an opportunist and a rascal, and one can
not help questioning the validity of his statements.

In other instances the playwrights openly condemn raillery by making
it the entertainment of fools. Although Congreve's Cynthia recognizes
that fools often have "all the jest in their persons, though they have
none in their conversation",[51] she objects when Lord and Lady Froth
begin to gossip about other people and rail at their acquaintances:
"Well, I find there are no fools so inconsiderable in themselves, but

[47] Molière, *L'École des femmes*, Act I, Scene 1.
[48] Congreve, *The Double Dealer*, p. 126.
[49] Congreve, *The Old Bachelor*, p. 86.
[50] Wycherly, *The Plain Dealer*, p. 394.
[51] Congreve, *The Double Dealer*, p. 153.

they can render other people contemptible by exposing their infirmities."[52]

Wycherly's *The Plain Dealer* contains a whole collection of contemptible "railers". Manly says that "a Fool, like a Coward, is the more to be fear'd behind a man's back, more than a witty Man: for, as a Coward is more bloody than a brave Man, a Fool is more malicious than a Man of wit."[53] Freeman finds pleasure "in laughing at Fools, and disappointing Knaves"[54] as does Novel who asks Olivia to be "allow'd a little Christian liberty of railing".[55] The rather uncharitable session, in which everyone is slandered, is also attended by Plausible and Olivia. Plausible uses a very special way of railing: he is a "Coxcomb, that speaks ill of all people a different way, and Libels every body with dull praise, and commonly in the wrong place, so makes his Panegyricks abusive Lampoons".[56] She most hypocritically pretends to hate the sport and tells her cousin that she will not even admit Novel because he is a fool "who, rather than not rail, will rail at the dead, whom none speak ill of".[57] Despite her statement, she invites Novel to her house and proposes a "little harmless railing".[58] It is Olivia who makes the most vicious comments about various people. After a while her cousin Eliza remarks to her: "So, Cousin, I find one may have a collection of all ones acquaintances Pictures as well at your house, as at Mr. Lely's; only the difference is, there we find 'em much handsomer than they are, and like: here, much uglier, and like: and you are the first of the profession of Picture-drawing I ever knew without flattery."[59]

Dorimant's mistress, Loveit, gives a very reasonable explanation why people like to amuse themselves at the expense of others: "You must allow that it is pleasanter to laugh at others than to be laughed at ourselves, though never so wittily."[60] Those who enjoy railing usually do not have the awareness and insight that they would do better to laugh at themselves and not at others. Hazlitt remarks that, "It is only very sensible or very honest people, who laugh as freely at their own absurdities as at those of their neighbours. In general the contrary rule

[52] *The Double Dealer*, p. 155.
[53] Wycherly, *The Plain Dealer*, p. 499.
[54] *The Plain Dealer*, p. 462.
[55] *The Plain Dealer*, p. 456.
[56] *The Plain Dealer*, p. 417.
[57] *The Plain Dealer*, p. 412.
[58] *The Plain Dealer*, p. 414.
[59] *Ibid.*
[60] Sir George Etherege, *Plays and Poems*, ed. and intro. A. Wilson Verity (London: John C. Nimmo, 1888), p. 348.

holds, and we only laugh at those misfortunes in which we are spectators, not sharers."[61]

Those who are capable of laughing at their own shortcomings usually manage to step beyond the boundary of folly. Many of the silly-wise fools can take a look at themselves and chuckle at their own foolishness. Even such a ridiculous character as Monsieur is able to joke about his absurd appearance. When he is forced to shed his fancy French attire and dress in Spanish clothes to please his future father-in-law, he perceives his ridiculousness. When his fiancee, Hippolita, teases him: "But where's your Spanish Beard, the thing of most consequence?"[62] Monsieur replies: "Jernie, do you tink Beards are as easie to be had as in de Play-houses, non; but if here be not the ugly-long-Spanish Beard, here are, I am certain, the ugly-long-Spanish Ear."[63]

Congreve is a great master in creating moments when men, both the foolish and the wise, take a fleeting look at themselves and chuckle at their own absurdities. Even such dunces as Sir Joseph Wittol and Sir Sampson have their moments of self-mockery. Those like Cynthia, Angelica, Mirabell and Millamant, who know the way of the world, who are aware of the shortcomings of others, are also able to see themselves and perceive with quiet amusement their idiosyncrasies and follies. Their merriment can be called humor in "its highest reaches", as it expresses "an outlook that resolves the incongruities of the world into enveloping harmony".[64]

Among those who are ignorant one finds the fools who enjoy practical jokes and the semi-fools who like to exercise their wit. According to Eastman a practical joke is "an elaborate, playful perpetration at the expense of someone not in the game",[65] and wit is nothing but "a practical joke played quickly, spontaneously, without too much self-and-other consciousness, and played upon the mind".[66] Miss Swabey distinguishes between wit and humor, stating that humor is,

... metaphysically deeper than wit. Whereas wit stands above life's battles, crowing like chantecleer over some men's victories and others' defeats;

---

[61]   William Hazlitt, *Lectures on the English Comic Writer* (New York: Doubleday and Company, 1966; first printing, 1819), p. 14.

[62]   Wycherly, *The Gentleman Dancing-Master*, p. 189.

[63]   *Ibid.*

[64]   Marie Collins Swabey, *Comic Laughter* (New Haven: Yale University Press, 1961), p. 93.

[65]   Max Eastman, *Enjoyment of Laughter* (New York: Simon and Schuster, 1936), p. 53.

[66]   Eastman, p. 54.

whereas it stands apart from the turmoil like a Micromegas or a Gulliver scoffing at the pettiness of human affairs, humor surpasses wit in its capacity, to be both immanent and transcendent in outlook, to enjoy both something like total perspective which reapportions the importance of things from an Olympian slant, and also humanly to share a vicarious intimacy with others. Humor introduces us to the hearts of our fellows, enabling us to compare others with ourselves and ourselves with them. Sometimes bacchanalian, never puritanically censorious, it accepts man's nature, its fleshly and spiritual mystery and, as beyond the shallows of mere fashion and convention. [67]

THE FOOL'S STRATAGEM: THE ABILITY TO INTRIGUE AND LEVELS OF INTELLIGENCE

In the world of drama the victors are able to plot and recognize intrigue when it is directed against them. They are often capable of succesfully disguising themselves and unmasking those who try to conceal their true identity. The victims, on the other hand, are the characters who are unable to perceive the intrigue around them and who do not have the intelligence to invent successful stratagems.

Jonson, in his *Volpone*, presents a complex hierarchy of plotters and disguisers whose place on the ladder of ignorance is clearly denoted by their ability to scheme. Mosca, Volpone's clever but evil servant, successfully disguises his true nature and outmaneuvres his master. Volpone, in his turn, manipulates with ease the greedy fortune-hunters Corvino, Corbaccio, and Corbone, and like a professional actor plays the role of a mountebank. The three birds of prey, on the other hand, are unsuccessfully plotting to inherit Volpone's wealth and their pretense to love and friendship for him is easily discerned by all. At the lowest level one finds the self-appointed master-spy, Sir PoliticWould-bee, dreaming up absurd intrigues, unable to see through his friend Peregrine's disguise and in turn disguising himself as a "most politic Tortoise". His wife, the fine Madame Would-bee, sees disguise where there isn't any when she suspects Peregrine to be a woman; also, she is foiled in her attempts to gain part of Volpone's money.

Jonson's and Molière's successful intriguers are often the clever servants. Restoration comedy also utilizes this type and one frequently encounters such characters as Dryden's Warner *(Sir Martin Mar-all)*, or Shadwell's Bridget *(The Humorists)* who direct the charade of fools through a merry confusion toward a complex but carefully planned

[67]   Swabey, *Comic Laughter*, p. 101.

conclusion. Congreve's maids and butlers often share in their masters' intrigues, as Jenny and Jeremy do in *Love for Love* and Mincing, Foible, and Waitwell in *The Way of the World*. However the great intriguers in Restoration comedy are not the servants but the masters, the true-wits, like Horner or Dorimant, who have the awareness which enables them to know and direct the rest of the characters.

Although the partially aware are frequently capable of plotting and outwitting the fools, in turn they are foiled by the masterminds of the comedy. The would-be-wits like Tattle (*Love for Love*) and the scheming women like Loveit (*The Man of Mode*) or the Lady Cockwood (*She Would if She Could*) belong to this group. A very special character is the one who, despite his mastering of intrigue and his awareness of pitfalls, is caught in a trap. Heartwell the old bachelor has escaped marriage all his life and tells his friends: "Marry quotha! I hope, in Heaven, I have a greater portion of grace, and I think I have baited too many of those traps to be caught in one myself."[68] He, like Molière's Arnolphe, is suspicious of everyone and avoids wedlock because he is afraid he may be deceived: "'Sdeath, I would not be a cuckold to e'er an illustrious whore in England!"[69] Despite all precautions Heartwell is caught. "O thou delicious, damned, dear, destructive woman! 'Sdeath, how the young fellows will hoot me! I shall be the jest of the town. Nay, in two days I expect to be chronicled in ditty, and sung in woeful ballad, to the tune of 'The Supperannuated Maiden's Comfort', or 'The Bachelor's Fall'; and on the third I shall be hanged in effigy, pasted up for the exemplary ornament of necessary-houses and clobblers' stalls."[70] By the end of the play he nearly marries an "illustrious whore" and is saved from disaster by his friends only at the last moment.

Among the fools one finds those whose intrigue is not only ineffective but who eventually become the victims of their own plots. Aphra Behn's Plottwell is ready to arrange everybody's happiness but his scheming backfires and he creates only confusion and disaster. Wycherly's comic character, Sir Simon Addleplot, "a Coxcomb always in pursuit of Women of Great Fortune",[71] believes that he is a great intriguer capable of making his own fortune by marrying a wealthy lady. He is Dapperwit's "cully", a rather lowly position, for Dapperwit himself is only a "little-Wit, a modest-wit" (p. 52).

---

[68] Congreve, *The Old Bachelor*, p. 50.
[69] *Ibid.*
[70] *The Old Bachelor*, p. 66.
[71] Wycherly, *Love in a Wood*, p. 9. Further references to this play are given in text, by page-numbers.

Sir Addleplot is always ready to join forces with anyone in plotting and he schemes not only with Dapperwit with whom he has been "partner in many an Intrigue" (p. 16) but also with Mrs. Joyner, a dishonest marriage broker and "bawd". She is aware of his vanity and stupidity and flatters him by saying that in intriguing "I am but a feeble instrument, you are the Engineer" (p. 16). With her help Addleplot desires to find a rich wife, and to make sure that he is successful, he thinks up a "double-plot" (p. 17). He'll court two ladies at the same time and thus he'll have "two strings to a Bow" (p. 17). The Widow Flippant he'll court by keeping his own identity, but Mrs. Martha he'll approach disguised as Jones, the clerk.

Sir Simon Addleplot disguises himself at times to find out who his enemies are (p. 61). But throughout the play, with or without his disguise, he is unable to distinguish friend from foe. Addleplot's disguise is ineffective and senseless and so are his intrigues. He brings a whole orchestra to St. James park where lovers meet and women wearing masks hunt for men. He explains that he had a good reason for engaging the musicians: "Frolick is not without intrigue, faith and troth; for I know the Fiddles will call the whole Herd of wizard Masks together; and then I discover a stray'd Mistress of mine be not amongst 'em" (p. 34).

The great schemer is confident from the very beginning that he'll at least win the Lady Flippant as, "Not treat, sweet words, good meen, but sly Intrigue / That must at length, the jilting Widow fegue" (p. 18). But even the lusty and willing widow proves to be something of a problem, and Sir Addleplot admits at one point that he is unable to "understand her tricks" (p. 34). He has, though, enough insight to know that "she is as arrant a Jilt, as ever pull's pillow from under husband's head" (p. 34).

The amusing seduction scene reveals the intelligence of both characters. The Widow Flippant encounters Sir Addleplot but does not recognize him in his disguise as Jones, the clerk. In the most obvious manner she attempts to seduce him, but Addleplot has difficulties perceiving her intentions. When she begs him: "Will you, Sir, will you?" he responds in a rather incongruous manner by presuming that she is a shy woman who needs some persuasion. He decides to overcome her scruples with complex intrigues: "I must have a plot for her, she is a coy woman" (p. 74). His plot succeeds in the shortest possible time, but the result is a mutual unmasking and disappointment. Such upsets do not discourage simple Sir Simon Addleplot, for even at the very end of the play, when he becomes the victim of his own intrigue, he states: "What, ruin'd by my own Plot, like an old Cavalier: yet like him too, I will plot on still" (p. 99).

Sir Addleplot is only a minor character in Wycherly's *Love in a Wood,* who like Sir Politic Wouldbee represents the lowest level of intrigue in a complex hierarchy of schemers. Dryden's Sir Martin Mar-all is, on the other hand, the main character of a comedy named after him and his magnificent incompetence sets the tone of the whole play.

Sir Martin Mar-all's clever servant, Warner, knows that his master is a "coxcomb, one that has no more brains than just those I carry for him".[72] He is a "confounded busie-brain" (p. 254) who like Sir Addleplot believes that he has a "fruitful Noodle filled with the most successfull intrigues" (p. 212). Though he is "so opinioned of his own Abilities, that he is ever designing somewhat", he "sows his strategems so shallow, that every Daw can pick 'em up" (p. 210).

Sir Martin Mar-all is incapable of plotting and when Warner attempts to help him and be a "godfather to a Fool" (p. 270) he foils his servant's plans and destroys his own chances to succeed. Sir Martin Mar-all desires to marry the lovely Millisent who is visiting the city in the company of her old-fashioned father. The aspiring suitor has not only to get the approval of the old country gentleman but also to eliminate a rival, Sir John Swallow.

When Sir Martin Mar-all first encounters Millisent's father he mistakes "the old man's humour" (p. 245) and offends him in all possible ways. Though he has to cope with the old man's displeasure the greater problem turns out to be Sir John Swallow. When the two suitors meet each other for the first time Sir Martin foolishly discloses all his plans and secrets to his rival. By revealing his stratagems, how he intends to woo and eventually marry Millisent, he gives the other beau the advantage to foil his plans. Warner is exasperated: "this was a Stratagem my shallow wit could ner'e have reach'd, to make a Confident of my Rival" (p. 218). The irony is wasted on Sir Martin who blames his failure on "unparallell'd Misfortune" (p. 218). Warner points out that it is due rather to "unparallell'd ignorance" (p. 218), and they have to think up ways to outwit Sir John Swallow.

Dryden establishes a pattern of behavior in the beginning of the play, a pattern which, with repetition, becomes more and more comic. The clever Warner invents a plan, Sir Martin Mar-all foils it, his servant is

---

[72] Dryden, *Sir Martin Mar-all* in *The Works of John Dryden*, Vol. IX, p. 210. Further references to this play are given in text, by page-numbers.

exasperated but recognizes that his master is a fool and it does not make sense to be "angry at what he cannot help" (p. 245). Warner tells Sir Martin Mar-all that he is a dunce, but then proceeds to think up new ways to further his master's cause. What saves this pattern from becoming entirely mechanical and artificial is Warner's attitude toward his master. He defends Sir Martin and helps him not only because he is well paid but also because he is genuinely fond of him. Their relationship, which resembles that of Don Quixote and Sancho Panza, eventually changes in the end of the play when Warner gives up in exasperation and even helps to foil his master.

In their intrigue against Sir John Swallow, Warner and Rose, Millisent's maid, attempt to find a way to get Sir Martin's rival out of town. Warner disguises his landlord as a postman and sends him to Sir John with a letter containing news about the demise of his father. The suitor is ready to leave, but Sir Martin Mar-all enters in time to unmask the false postman and save his rival from treachery. Warner, saddened by his master's stupidity, remarks: "You have so little Brains, that a Penn'-orth of Butter melted under 'um, would set 'um afloat" (p. 235). Warner is ready to leave his master but then for a price reconsiders his decision. He pretends to have a fight with Sir Martin and afterwards enters the service of Sir John to keep an eye on developments.

On Millisent's and Sir John's wedding-day, Warner offers to take the bride to the church, but in reality he intends to bring her to Sir Martin Mar-all. Sir Martin meanwhile dreams up his own plot and writes an anonymous letter to Millisent's father warning him that the bride will be waylaid as she goes to church. Millisent is kept home and when Sir Martin encounters his servant he boasts about his infinitely clever stratagem: "Hereafter, Warner, be it known unto thee, I will endure no more to be thy May-game: thou shalt no more dare to tell me, I spoil thy projects, and discover thy designs; for I have play'd such a Prize, without thy help, of my own Motherwit ('tis true I am hasty sometimes, and so do harm; but when I have a mind to shew my self, there's no man in England, though I say't, comes near me as to point of imagination) I'le make thee acknowledge I have laid a Plot that has soul in't" (p. 253).

Warner informs his master that he has just spoiled an excellent intrigue. To discourage Sir John Swallow from marrying Millisent, Warner tells the bridegroom that his bride is not an innocent virgin but has known several men before him. Sir John is ready to abandon Millisent for a pure, artless girl, but the quixotic knight, Sir Martin Mar-all, appears just in time to defend the honor of his lady-love. He not only assures Sir John Swallow that Millisent's honor is unsoiled but also beats Warner for spreading evil rumors. Warner decides after this experience that he has had enough, but after lengthy persuasion is willing to make a last effort. Sir Martin Mar-all complains that their stratagems fail because he is not informed of all the plans and does not know what is happening. He asks Warner: "Next time make me of your Counsel, let me enter into the business, instruct me in every point, and then if I discover all, I am resolv'd to give over affairs, and retire from the world" (p. 266).

The last intrigue does not involve Sir John Swallow, but Millisent. Though Warner has tried to convince her that his master is a very exceptional wit who is not only clever but also "speaks French, sings, dances, plays upon the lute" (p. 269), she begins to suspect that Sir Martin Mar-all is a fool. She wants proof of his excellence and would like to be serenaded by him. Warner, who knows that his master "sings like a Scritch-Owle" and can't play a musical instrument instructs him: ". . . get up into your Window, and set two Candles by you, take my Land-lords Lute in your hand, and fumble on't, and make grimmaces with your mouth, as if you sung; in the mean time, I'le play in the next Room in the dark, and consequently your Mistress, who will come to her Balcone over against you, will think it to be you; and at the end of every Tune, I'le ring the Bell that hangs between your Chamber and mine, that you may know when to have done" (p. 271).

Warner plays the lute and sings but Sir Martin Mar-all has not enough sense to stop "making grimmaces with his mouth" at the end of the song. Millisent recognizes that her suitor is a fool and that Warner is the accomplished wit and gallant. After some elaborate schemes, when most of the characters disguise themselves, the fools who can't plot or recognize disguise become the victims. Sir Martin Mar-all marries Millisent's maid, Rose, and Sir John Swallow, who likes pure and innocent maidens, weds a pregnant young woman who bears the child of another man. Warner, who at last fends for himself, marries Millisent.

Sir Martin Mar-all and Addleplot are rather artificial characters mainly because the act of plotting itself is removed from reality and is part of the contrived world of drama. The characters who use disguise are frequently "unnatural" too and belong to the realm of make-believe.

Physical disguise is most of the time unconvincing and serves only to deceive those who are particularly blind and foolish. The limitations

of these characters are not only exposed when they are unable to recognize a masked person but also when they attempt to disguise themselves and are recognized for what they are. Physical disguise is usually
part of farce and low comedy, but mental disguise belongs to a more
subtle kind of drama. To recognize pretention and discern the true
nature of a man requires not only a perceptive eye but also a keen
mind.

Disguise is not too often used in Restoration comedy, despite the
fact that masks were frequently worn by the ladies during their visits
to the theatre, to social occasions, and even on their evening-strolls
through the parks. Occasionally one finds also in the comedies characters who don their vizards and, like Mistress Flippant and her friend
Lydia, walk through the park, one to pick up a man, the other to find
out the truth about her faithless lover. In Etherege's *She Would if She
Could,* two young ladies, Ariana and Gatty, newly arrived from the
country and delighted with city-ways, wear "vizard-masks" as they
saunter through fashionable Mulberry-Garden. They flirt with two of
the gallants who eventually try to persuade them to remove their
masks:

Courtall.   These were pretty toys, invented first for the good of us poor
            lovers to deceive the jealous and to blind the malicious; but
            the proper use is so wickedly perverted, that it makes all honest
            men hate the fashion mortally.[73]

In the intrigue and unmasking that follows at times the gallants are the
victims, and at other times the young girls become the butts of laughter.
The society-game of wearing a vizard is usually played by those who
are partially aware, and the comedy which ensues is light-hearted and
often goodnatured.

Disguise is also used by the playwrights to facilitate the conclusion
of a play. In *Sir Martin Mar-all,* Millisent and Rose exchange costumes
and thus the imperceptive fools marry the wrong women. In Congreve's
Love for Love, Tattle, who aspires to marry the beautiful and witty
Angelica, and Mrs. Frail, who plots to catch Valentine for a husband,
are tricked by the machination of Jeremy the butler. He disguises Mrs.
Frail as Angelica, and Tattle as Valentine and manages to marry them
to each other. The particular irony of this deception is that both characters are sufficiently aware to disguise themselves effectively but too
blind to recognize the other under a mask.

[73]   Etherege, *Plays and Poems,* p. 142.

It is rather exceptional when the fools wear the disguise, as in the case of Sir Politic Wouldbee or Tattle. Usually the master-schemer wears the mask and manipulates the unsuspecting fool without being recognized. Wycherly shows the gradually increasing awareness of Margery Pinchwife by showing her growing ability to intrigue and finally by enabling her to disguise herself successfully. In the beginning of the play she is a naive and unsophisticated young country woman, the victim of a suspicious domineering husband, but as she grows more aware of the ways of the world and the city, she learns to outwit her watchful spouse. When the jealous Pinchwife shuts her in the house, she disguises herself in the attire of her sister-in-law and unrecognized by her husband is led by him to Horner, her lover. The initial roles are reversed and the cunning Mrs. Pinchwife has become the master-intriguer.

Impersonation is another form of disguise often used in comedy. When Mirabell's servant Waitwell is ordered to court Lady Wishfort, he disguises himself as the gallant suitor Sir Rowland. Mrs. Wishfort, blinded by her desire for a husband, cannot perceive the deception and becomes the victim of the plot directed against her. Also, in Farquhar's *The Beaux's Stratagem* two young men, Aimwell and Archer, who are down on their luck, take turns in playing the role of the master and the servant to give the illusion of wealth to prospective victims. After Aimwell meets the girl he wishes to marry he assumes a title and position to which he has no right and presents himself as Lord Viscount Aimwell.

Impersonation is only a step away from pretension, the "mental disguise" with its infinite varieties and possibilities. To deceive others and gain their ends wanton ladies pretend to be virtuous, rogues to be honest, and foes to be friends. Whereas physical disguise and impersonation are to be found usually in lighthearted comedy, pretension, with its moral implications, is part of the darker, satiric plays of Restoration drama.

Wycherly's comedies are teeming with pretenders to virtue, honor, and holiness. Some of his characters are successful in disguising their natures, as Mr. Horner is, whose suddenly gained virtue is a sham, while others are seen through without difficulty, like his hypocrites, Gripe and Olivia. One of Wycherly's deeply ironic unmaskings occurs in *The Country Wife,* when the three pretenders to virtue, Lady Fidget, Mrs. Dainty Fidget, and Mrs. Squeamish consume a few bottles of wine and disclose their true natures. After Mrs. Dainty proposes, "let

us throw our Masques over our heads",[74] Lady Fidget confides in
Horner and tells him that their pretention to virtue permits them to
misbehave freely. Mrs. Squeamish does not hesitate to elaborate on
the subject: "Demureness, Coyness, and Modesty that you see in our
Faces in the Boxes at Plays, is as much a sign of a kind woman, as a
Vizard-mask in the Pit."[75] Mrs. Dainty agrees that those women who
are "kind" and only too willing are the ones who pretend to be the
most virtuous.

Dainty.	For I assure you, women are least mask'd, when they have the Velvet Vizard on.
Lady Fidget.	You wou'd have found us modest women in our denyals only.
Squeamish.	Our bashfulness is only the reflection of the Men's.
Dainty.	We blush, when they are shame-fac'd.
Horner.	I beg your pardon Ladies, I was deceiv'd in you devilishly, but why, that mighty pretence to Honour?
Lady Fidget.	We have told you; but sometimes 'twas for the same reason you pretend business often, to avoid ill company, to enjoy the better, and more privately those you love.

The three ladies are defeated by Horner, whose stratagem, though
amoral as theirs, happens to be somewhat more original and complex.
The mixture of awareness and ignorance, the blend of crude honesty,
blatant pretension, and lack of any perception of morals, makes the
unmasking a dark but dramatic experience. The ladies are not only the
victims of the dominating Horner but also of their own moral ignorance.

Stratagem of any sort plays a major role in Restoration comedy, not
only because in many of the plays plot is more important than characterization or theme but, also, as Aeschylus discovered, schemes
which are disclosed to the audience and characters who are disguised
heighten the dramatic irony of the play. Moreover these playwrights
cater to an audience which consists of arch-schemers: the courtiers of
Charles the Second, and their ladies who were only too eager to engage
in intrigues. Consequently the stage, most of the time, reflects the attitude of the audience and the master-plotters become the most delightful and engaging individuals of the play.

Congreve creates schemers who are most of the time intelligent and
charming people, whereas Wycherly's puppet-masters are often unpleasant and amoral. Wycherly, as Jonson did before him, seems to

---

[74]   Wycherly, *The Country Wife*, p. 349.
[75]   *The Country Wife*, p. 351.

suggest in his comedies that plotting has its unsavory aspects. His good characters either stay out of intrigues as Alithea does, or like Fidelia, who disguises herself as a boy to serve her beloved Manly, are most reluctant to scheme.

Though playwrights may have different attitudes toward the master-plotters they seem to agree that the dunces are inevitably those who can't think up, carry out, or perceive a good stratagem.

HAPPY SLAVERY: IGNORANCE OF SELF

Lord Froth and his wife take great pride in loving each other and they demonstrate their affection publicly whenever they can. Lady Froth compares Cynthia's beau, Mellefont, to her husband and tries to convince the girl that her husband has much more "solemnity yet complaisance" than the young man has.[76] Cynthia defends her suitor:

Cynthia.   He does not indeed affect either pertness or formality, for which I like him. Here he comes.

Lady Froth.   And my lord with him; pray observe the difference. (Enter Lord Froth, Mellefont, and Brisk.)

Cynthia.   (Aside) Impertinent creature! I could almost be angry with her.

Lady Froth.   My lord, I have been telling Cynthia how much I have been in love with you, I swear I have; I'm not ashamed to own it now. Ah, it makes my heart leap! I vow, I sigh when I think on't; my dear lord, ha! ha! ha! do you remember my lord? (Squeezes him by the hand, looks kindly on him, sighs and then laughs out.)

Lord Froth.   Pleasant creature! perfectly well, – Ah, that look! ay, there it is! who could resist? 'twas so my heart was made a captive first, and ever since 't has been in love with happy slavery.

Lady Froth.   O that tongue! that dear deceitful tongue! that charming softness in your mien and your expression! and then your bow! Good my lord, bow as you did when I gave you my picture. – (Gives him a pocket-glass.) Pray mind, my lord; ah, he bows charmingly! – Nay, grow jealous, I vow now. (He bows profoundly low, then kisses the glass.)

Lord Froth.   I saw myself there, and kissed it for your sake.

Lady Froth.   Ah, gallantry to the last degree![77]

---

[76]   Congreve, *The Double Dealer*, p. 132.
[77]   *The Double Dealer*, pp. 132-133.

Lord Froth, who kisses his own reflection in the mirror, and Lady Froth, who is enchanted by her own image, are extreme examples of comic characters whose self-love blinds them to their own natures. They see an idealized, illusory picture of themselves, not only in the mirror but also in the eyes of other people. Cynthia is aware of their true nature and when Lord Froth turns to her with the question: "Don't you think us a happy couple?"[78] she gives a diplomatic answer.

Cynthia.   I vow my lord, I think you are the happiest couple in the world; for you're not only happy in one another and when you are together, but happy in yourselves, and by your-selves.

Lord Froth does not sense the irony in Cynthia's reply but takes it as a compliment. He remarks:

Lord Froth.   I hope Mellefont will make a good husband too.
Cynthia.   'Tis my interest to believe he will, my lord.
Lord Froth.   D'ye think he'll love you as well as I do my wife?
Cynthia.   I believe he'll love me better.
Lord Froth.   Heavens! that can never be; but why do you think so?
Cynthia.   Because he has not so much reason to be fond of himself.[79]

Congreve's presentation of Lord Froth's self-love is amusing and even charming. Not all authors are as tolerant toward those who fail to know themselves as Congreve is. Socrates laughs at times at those who live an unexamined life and are ignorant of their own natures. Other times he is exasperated with them and condemns their inflexibility and un-willingness to improve themselves. Shakespeare seems to be deeply concerned with this problem and presents both the tragic and comic sides of ignorance of self. Lear, who has but "slenderly known" him-self, learns, and, as he gains insight and humility, his stature grows and his humanity increases. Malvolio, on the other hand, blinded by pride and the conviction that he is attractive and important, becomes more and more ridiculous as his inflexibility and delusions become evident. He, like other comic characters who are too limited to perceive the discrepancy between the real self and the illusory one, becomes the target of ridicule. Such fools are frequently depicted in Restoration comedy. Some believe that they are beautiful, generous, lovable; others pride themselves for being clever, witty, and knowledgeable.

Many of Shadwell's humor characters are dunces who never doubt that they are outstanding people. Drybob, one of the fools from *The*

[78] *The Double Dealer*, p. 133.
[79] *Ibid.*

Humorists, believes that he is witty and honest. He thinks that he can sing, tell wonderful jokes, and also that he is appreciated by all. "The ladies of the Town are so exorbitantly pleas'd with my manner of speaking, that I have been often set upon to speak *ex tempore* to a whole Room full, and have ravish'd 'em all for half an hour together; and this I have got by University Learning and Travelling." [80] Drybob's friend, Crazy, believes also that he is so charming that all the ladies are in love with him. When a young woman confides in him and tells about her love for another man, Crazy prefers to interpret her statement as a love-declaration for him. He finds it not at all surprising that he is adored and remarks casually: "Well! 'tis most evident, she has a passion for me, but who can help it." [81]

Among Shadwell's plays, *The Sullen Lovers* is perhaps the one which contains the greatest variety of fools whose "humour" is self-love and blindness to their own natures. Shadwell aimed at subordinating "Plott and Business" to characterization and succeeded as he set out to "hold up the Humour" of each personage in the play.[82]

The "Plott and Business" of the play is uncomplicated. The gay and witty Lovel is in love with Caroline, who is "of the same Humour with Love" (p. 15). The young man has a friend, Stanford, who is a misanthrope, "A Morose Melancholy Man, tormented beyond Measure with the Impertinence of People, and resolved to leave the World to be quit of them" (p. 14). Caroline has a sister, Emilia, who is "of the same Humour with Stanford" (p. 15). The carefree and witty couple schemes to bring the two misanthropes together. They are helped by Roger, Lovel's servant, who also happens to be witty and cunning. The three fools of the play, a "brace of Jack-Puddens", according to Stanford, are the fantastic Sir Positive At-all, "a foolish Knight, that pretends to understand every thing in the world, and will suffer no man to understand any thing in his Company; so foolishly Positive, that he will never be convinced of an Error, though never so grosse" (p. 14), Ninny, a "conceited Poet" (p. 14), and Woodcock, "a Familiar Coxcombe, that embraces and kisses all men" (p. 14).

Shadwell presents a double vision of folly throughout his play. Stanford and Emilia are exasperated by stupidity and are contemptuous of the duces who intrude on their privacy, whereas Lovel and Caroline

---

[80]   Shadwell, *The Humorists,* p. 243.
[81]   *The Humorists,* p. 241.
[82]   Shadwell, *The Sullen Lovers,* p. 10. Further references to this play are given in text, by page-numbers.

are amused and entertained by their behavior. To laugh at fools, "this is my recreation" (p. 27), states Lovel, and Caroline echoes his attitude when she says that they "afford me so much recreation that I do not know how I should laugh without them" (p. 31). Bitter rejection and amused and good-natured acceptance of folly are both voiced in this comedy. It seems that Shadwell's own attitude must have been not unlike Stanford's. He creates Sir Positive At-all because he is upset and highly irritated with unbending and ignorant fools. He states in the Preface to *The Sullen Lovers*:

I must confess it is very ungenerous to accuse those that modestly confess their Errors; but positive Men, that justifie all their faults, are common Enemies, that no man ought to spare, prejudical to all Societies they live in, destructive to all Communication, always endeavoring Magisterially to impose upon our Understandings, against the Freedome of Mankind: These ought no more to be suffer'd amongst us than wild beasts: for no corrections that can be laid upon 'em are of power to reforme 'em; and certainly it was a positive Foole that Solomon spoke of, when he said, "bray him in a Mortar, and yet he will retain his folly." (p. 11)

The "positive Foole" of the play believes that he is modest, yet that he is the "man of the most universal knowledge of any man in England". Everybody, including Ninny and Woodcock, knows that he is not only ignorant of all the knowledge he presumes to possess but that he is also ignorant of what he is. The comic truth is often suggested by Sir Positive himself. He incorporates in his speeches passages which, ironically, indicate his true nature. "I am an Ass, an Ideot, a Blockhead, and a Rascal, if I don't understand Dramatique Poetry of all things in the World" (p. 42). He is not only a connoisseur of drama but also writes plays. When he praises his last creation, "The Lady in the Lobster" (p. 53), he ends his eulogy with: "And let me tell you, Sir, if in any Dramatic Poem there has been such breaks, such Characters, such Figures, such Intrigues, such Surprizes, such Fire, Salt, and Flame, then I am no Judge: I understand nothing in this World" (p. 51).

Sir Positive is not only an expert in literature, but also in art and music. He believes that he can identify and judge the paintings of any great master and when he is shown a picture he swears that it is a "Hans Holbins" (p. 71). Caroline enlightens the judge of fine art: "Why 'tis a new Sign for my Landlord, finish'd but yesterday, that cost him a Noble the painting, done by a Fellow that paints Posts and Railes, one Humphrey Hobson" (p. 71). As for music: "if any Man in England gives you a better account of that then I do, I will give all Mankind leave to spit upon me" (p. 25), states Sir Positive.

The all-knowing knight speaks Greek and Latin, understands ship-building and knows so much about law that, as he says, "the greatest Lawyers in England come to me for advice in matters of difficulty" (pp. 60-61). When Stanford merely mentions the word mankind, Sir Positive interrupts him with: "Mankind! Dost thou know what thou say'st now? do'st thou talk of Mankind? I am confident thou never so much thought'st of Mankind in thy life; I'le tell thee, I will give Dogs leave to piss upon me, if any Man understands Mankind better then myself, now you talk of that. I have consider'd all Mankind, I have thought of nothing else but Mankind this Moneth" (p. 27).

Sir Positive's expertise becomes even more absurd when he professes to know matters which are certainly not to his credit. When Ninny mentions the word pimp, Sir Positive declares himself a master of the profession: "Why there is not a Lady of Pleasure from Blackwell to Tuttle-Fields that I am not intimately acquainted with, nay that I do not know the state of her Body from the first entering into the Calling" (p. 40). He also proudly announces that for debauching women "I am the greatest son of a Whore in the World if any one comes near me" (p. 41). Sir Positive boasts that he does not only excel in cheating at card-games but also that he is mad: "I 'scaped Bedlam very narrowly, 'tis not above a twelve-moneth since my brains were settled again" (p. 43).

Anyone who professes to know a subject is immediately attacked by the knight who can't tolerate people who might know something better than he does. In a hilarious scene, while Ninny beats false time and Woodcock dances to one of Sir Positive's compositions, a "corrant", the proud composer turns to Stanford and wonders if he enjoys the performance.

Sir Positive.	Here's a Corrant for you, ha! Stanford, what thinks't of this?
Woodcock.	Think quoth a', I think I danc'd it as well As any Man in England, Bully-Rock.
Lovel.	Certainly, Sir Positive, he dances very finely.
Sir Positive.	As any Man that ever was born upon two Leggs: I defie any Man in the World that out-does him; For betwixt you and I, I taught him every step he has. (p. 26)

When Woodcock declares that he knows mathematics and Ninny states that he can play the cittern Sir Positive belittles Woodcock and tells Ninny: "You talke of a Cittern before me? when I invented the instrument?" (p. 71). After such an upsetting experience Sir Positive becomes even more ruffled when Lovel and Caroline express their doubts about his knowledge of various subjects. They tease him by questioning his claim to be as great a statesman as Mazarin, of knowing metaphysics, of being able to perform rope-dancing tricks and even of baking a good pastry. Sir Positive is driven to distraction and, after he recites frenziedly an absurd catalog of subjects he knows to perfection, he leaves the amused company.

Sir Positive cannot bear even the suggestion of criticism or correction. His first reaction to an uncomplimentary remark is the stock-rationalization of every fool; either he takes the remark for "railing" or blames the other person, accusing him of stupidity and ignorance. The moment he presumes that someone actually dares to find fault with him he becomes vengeful. When Sir Positive suspects a little clerk, who attended the performance of his play, of not liking his creation, he challenges him to a fight. The timid Timothy Scribble assures the knight that he liked "The Lady in the Lobster" and that he does not desire to duel with the author. To appease the irate Sir Positive the clerk has to sign an absurd document.

Clerk.	(read) I do acknowledge and firmly believe that the Play of Sir Positive At-all Knight, called the Lady in the Lobster, nowithstanding it was damn'd by the Malice of the Age, shall not only read, but it shall act with any of Ben Johnsons, and Beaumont's and Fletcher's plays.
Sir Positive.	Hold! hold! I'll have Shakespeares in, 'slife I had like to have forgot that.
Clerk.	(read) With all my heart.
	I do likewise hereby attest that he is no purloiner of other mens Work, the general fame and opinion nowithstanding. and that he is a Poet, Mathematician, Divine, Statesman, Lawyer, Phisitian, Geographer, Musician, and indeed a **Unus in Omnibus** through all Arts and Sciences, and hereunto I have set my hand. (p. 53)

There comes a moment even in Sir Positive At-all's life when he has to admit – if not to the world, then at least to himself – that he is unable to fathom certain matters. After he is tricked into marrying a pregnant lady of questionable virtue, he seems to be baffled and admits: "Well! this is the first thing in the World that I have met with which I did not understand: but I am resolv'd, I'le not acknowledge that: Master Lovell, I knew well enough what I did when I marry'd her, He's a wise man that marry's a harlot, he's on the surest side, who but an Ass would marry at uncertainty?" (p. 91).

The discrepancy between what Sir Positive is and what he believes himself to be is very great. Consequently he remains throughout the play an absurd and artificial character. Woodcock and Ninny, the other two fools who lack self-awareness, are still stylized humor characters but less grossly drawn than the all-knowing knight.

Woodcock fancies himself to be a great poet and a musician. His constant companion, Ninny, is of a different opinion. When a lady wonders if the gentleman she met is a poet, he remarks: "Woodcock a poet? a pimp, is he not?" (p. 40). Stanford recalls him without enthusiasm as "That familiar Loving Puppy Woodcock, that admires Fooles for Wits, and torments me with a damned Coranto, as he calls it, upon his Violin, which he us'd So barbariously, I was ready to take it for a Bag-pipe" (p. 21). Woodcock's frequent visits upset Stanford who abhors the poet's enthusiastic greetings: "Let me kiss thee Dear Heart; 'gad I had rather kiss thee than any Woman" (p. 35). Also to please his host, the affable Woodcock echoes Stanford's misanthropic complaints. He commiserates with him about the state of the world and offers to keep him company when he retires from it. "Ah, how we shall enjoy ourselves when we are both together, how we shall despise the rest of the World, Dear Heart" (p. 36). Woodcock is unaware that it is his folly which drives Stanford to distraction and further annoys him by complaining about "the Idle Fellows that thrust themselves into Company", bothering everyone present. Woodcock realized neither that he has just told the comic truth about himself, nor that he has mocked and enraged the humorless Stanford.

Ninny, like his friend Woodcock, considers others to be fools and himself to be the wisest man in the world. He fancies that he is a great poet and forces everyone to listen when he recites his creations. Stanford considers his verses to be "nothing but a Jingling of words" (p. 24). Ninny, like Sir Positive, interprets insult as "raillery" and is outraged when his poetry is not appreciated. He complains about the bookseller, "an Ignorant ingrateful Fellow" (p. 38), because he refuses to publish his works.

Both Woodcock and Ninny become the victims of a plot which further reveals the extent of their self-love and folly. Roger, the instigator of the scheme, employs the same intrigue which makes Malvolio ridiculous in Shakespeare's *Twelfth Night*. Each dunce is told that Emilia is in love with him. As both are convinced that they are attractive and talented, they do need not much persuasion to accept he good news and proceed to charm Emilia with their performances. Ninny who believes that she loves his poetry reads to her his verses, and Woodcock who thinks that she is enamored in his voice sings to her his compositions. It takes a long time and all of Emila's wit to persuade them that their artistic efforts are not appreciated.

Even though disappointments momentarily stun Sir Positive, Woodcock, and Ninny, their confidence is quickly restored by flattery. Roger capitalizes on their inordinate vanity by complimenting them whenever he finds an opportunity. For such service he is highly appreciated and receives not only praises but also money. Lovel also flatters the fools. He does it only for entertainment as he realizes that criticism would not enable them to change, but would only serve to upset and enrage them. The three dunces constantly praise each other. It is obvious that in exchange they expect compliments for their own accomplishments.

Ninny and Woodcock are drawn as exaggerated humor characters, but when Shadwell portrays Stanford and Emilia he uses more subtle ways. He not only diminishes the distance between their illusory and real selves, thus creating more lifelike characters, but he also uses more sophisticated methods to show their shortcomings.

The self-love of the three fools is conveyed in a rather straightforward manner. Sir Positive is solely occupied with his achievements, Ninny is drunk with the sound of his own poetry and when Woodcock is asked to make a comment about his friend's music he can only praise his own dancing. Though Emilia and Stanford are much more intelligent than the "brace of Jack-Puddens", they are still mainly preoccupied with themselves and lack self-knowledge.

When the two misanthropes meet they are locked together in a room by the scheming Lovel who wants them to get acquainted. The stage-directions indicate that "Stanford and Emilia walk up and down, and take little notice of another" (p. 37). Their dialogues turn out to be monologues on the evil nature of man and the world. The two lovers never seem to discover each other and when they fall in love they seem to adore only their own mirror-images. Lord Froth professes to love his wife, yet kisses only his own reflection; similarly Stanford and Emilia become enamored of their own image and their approval of each other is merely a praise of their own ways of thinking and behaving.

After Lovel encounters Emilia for the first time and listens to her complaints, he is delighted: "O rare! Stanford, here's just thy counterpart To a hair." Throughout the play the two misanthropes voice exactly the same thoughts and respond in the same way to people and events. Their favorite word is "impertinent", an expression which covers any person, trait or behavior which displeases them. It is impertinent to joke, to scheme, to wear fashionable clothes or even go to the theatre. Folly is impertinent and so are the dunces who disturb their solitude. Ironically Stanford, who was upset when Woodcock echoed his thoughts, is delighted when Emilia does the same thing. He eventually even manages to come up with a compliment: "I must needs confess I never saw any Woman I dislik'd less" (p. 82).

As the three Jack-Puddens never realize that they are not the greatest men in England, so Stanford and Emilia do not fathom that their negative view is wrong and that the greatest "impertinence" is their sullen and objectionable behavior. Caroline is aware that they will find "impertinence" in everybody else but never in themselves and the clever Roger is of the same opinion. Lovel and his servant easily manipulate the sullen lovers throughout the play, just as they do with the rest of the fools. By the end of the play everybody is unchanged, as ignorant as before and perhaps just a little bit happier.

According to Socrates, an unexamined life is not worth living. Congreve's Cynthia thinks otherwise. At first when she contemplates the ignorance of Lady and Lord Froth she contemptuously calls them fools. Then, after some reflection, she reconsiders her statement: "Why should I call 'em fools? the world thinks better of 'em; for these have quality and education, wit and fine conversation, are received and admired by the world: – if not, they like and admire themselves. And why not that true wisdom, for 'tis happiness? and for aught I know, we have misapplied the name all this while, and mistaken the thing; since –

> If happiness in self-content is placed,
> The wise are wretched, and fools only blessed.[83]

---

[83] Congreve, *The Double Dealer*, pp. 156-157.

IV

FIELDS OF IGNORANCE AND KNOWLEDGE (II)

DIAN'S BUD O'ER CUPID'S FLOWER: KNOWLEDGE OF OTHERS

Because Titania did not comply with his wishes, Oberon decides to torment her. He bids Puck to fetch a little Western flower which, "will make or man or woman madly dote / Upon the next live creature that it sees."[1] The vindictive fairy-king carefully plots his revenge:

> Having once this juice,
> I'll watch Titania when she is asleep
> And drop the liquor of it in her eyes
> The next thing then she waking looks upon,
> Be it on lion, bear, or wolf, or bull,
> On meddling monkey or a busy ape,
> She shall pursue it with the soul of love.[2]

The juice of the little Western flower blinds Titania to reality and makes her dote on the grotesque Bottom who, thanks to Puck's magic, is endowed with an ass's head. To the enchanted fairy-queen his ridiculous appearance seems beautiful, his rustic song the loveliest music, and his silly remarks the greatest wisdom. She lavishes all her tenderness on monster-Bottom who in turn never perceives the fairy-loveliness of the queen. He is solely concerned with his own welfare and notices neither his transformation nor the airy magic which surrounds him.

Oberon eventually takes pity on Titania and decides to release her "charmed eye" from "monster view".[3] He uses a new potion and pours the juice of "Dian's bud o'er Cupid's flower"[4] to free the queen from her enchantment. After Titania awakens, the memory of Bottom seems

---

[1] William Shakespeare, *A Midsummer Night's Dream*, II.1., 171-172.
[2] *A Midsummer Night's Dream*, II.1, 176-182.
[3] *A Midsummer Night's Dream*, III.2., 376-377.
[4] *A Midsummer Night's Dream*, IV.1., 76.

like a nightmare to her: "What visions have I seen! / Methought I was enamored of an ass." [5]

The temporary blindness of the fairy-queen brought about by the magic of love and the permanent sightlessness of the rustic weaver are extreme examples of the inability to see other people and recognize them for what they are. Titania's charmed vision which transforms an ass into a princely lover is caused by love, whereas Bottom's blindness is due to his inherent and incurable stupidity. In one instance the discrepancy which exists between Titania's vision and the reality creates comedy and in the other the source of amusement is Bottom's fantastic lack of perception. Romantic comedy frequently deals with blindness brought about by love, but the writer of Restoration drama does not depict it in his plays.

Awareness of others is a prerequisite for success in a world which is teeming with pretention and deception. The Restoration rakes have no mercy on starry-eyed innocents whose vision is clouded by romantic dreams. The only kind of woman who is capable of succeeding is the one who can size up a man, take into consideration all his virtues and weaknesses, outwit him in his attempts to seduce her, yet love him deeply despite her clear knowledge of his nature. The great heroines who succeed in marrying the men of their choices, Congreve's Cynthia, Angelica, and Millamant, Etherege's Harriet and Wycherly's Hippolita, are all women of supreme awareness.

Love is an accidental power which blinds man to the nature of another being, and the same is true for skillful deception. This is the cause for most misunderstandings in Restoration comedy. Congreve is keenly aware of the power of the villain and dissimulator who uses the guise of a kind and benevolent friend. In his Dedication to *The Double Dealer* he defends one of his characters, Mellefont, whom the critics berated for being gullible and not too bright. Mellefont does not recognize Maskwell's evil nature and believes that the villain is his friend. Congreve defends his hero by stating that: "If an open-hearted honest man, who has the entire confidence in one whom he takes to be his friend, and whom he has obliged to be so; and who (to confirm his opinion) in all appearance, and upon several trials has been so; if this man be deceived by the treachery of the other, must he of necessity commence fool immediately, only because the other proved a villain?" [6]

---

[5] *A Midsummer Night's Dream*, IV.1., 79-80.
[6] William Congreve, Dedication to *The Double Dealer* in *Complete Plays*, ed. Alexander Charles Ewald (New York: Hill and Wang, 1964), p. 117.

Beside the accidental forces which make fools of perfectly sensible men, one finds those individuals who were born blind and never managed to gain any insight into others.

Inherent stupidity, as in the case of Shakespeare's rustic weaver, limits the perception of an individual. Many fools, like Bottom, are so preoccupied with themselves that they fail to take notice of anyone else. Sir Positive at-All, of Shadwell's *The Sullen Lovers,* has not time for anyone but himself. The rest of humanity only exists to notice his greatness and to applaud his excellence. Ignorance of others as in the case of Pirandello's plays has often tragic overtones. The fictitious personages of his *Six Characters in Search of an Author* are aware that they are locked into their little world and are not capable of understanding other men. Their knowledge brings sorrow and frustration whereas the unawareness of the common fool enables him to exist in a blissful and self-imposed solitude. In his little world there is no one to doubt his all-engulfing importance or disturb his self-confidence.

In Restoration comedy many characters are preoccupied with themselves. The fop seldom notices anyone else and is only eager to see himself wherever he goes. He looks for a mirror in every room so that he can admire his own, flattering image. Similarly, people like Congreve's Lord Froth look for the reflection of their image in the eyes of others and remain unaware of their fellow men. Shadwell's "sullen lovers" fall in love because they are like twins, beloved mirror-images of their own natures.

Some are willing to look beyond themselves, but they behold the rest of humanity through distorting glasses. A comic character often projects some of his traits into others and attributes his own predilections to his fellow men. Mr. Pinchwife, suspecting everyone's motives, is afraid of being cuckolded because he himself is dishonorable and devious. Pinchwife has another flaw which prevents him from ever understanding his wife. His vision is limited by his belief in theories. Like Molière's tyrant, Arnolphe, he also has preconceived ideas about marriage and the education of wives. Like all dogmatists he shapes people to suit his theories instead of examining their true selves. Molière's heroes are often riddled with obsessions which do not allow them to judge their fellow men. The classical example is Orgon whose adoration of Tartuffe prevents him from seeing even the most obvious flaws.

The vision of a man can also be curtailed by other factors. There are universally accepted relations between men which lend themselves to comic misunderstandings. In the battle of sexes the warriors often complain about the inscrutability of their opponents. Congreve's suitors, such as Valentine and Mirabell, are puzzled by the ways of women and find the opposite sex charming, desirable, but also mysterious. The husbands of Restoration comedy fare even worse and seem to be notoriously ignorant of their wives' natures. The procession of cuckolds testifies to their gullibility and their lack of perception. Wycherly's Sir Jasper never suspects that his wife is anything but virtuous, and Pinchwife suspects but is deceived. Etherege's Sir Oliver Cockwood escapes cuckoldom not because he is in any way aware of his spouse's nature but because the young man Lady Cockwood singled out for her attention is unwilling to comply with her wishes.

Not only difference in sex but also difference in age facilitates misunderstanding. The "generation gap" produces many of the stock-characters of comedy. The foolish and often authoritarian father who does not know his children and is victimized by them is a well-known figure in Restoration comedy. Wycherly's cunning Hippolita meets her lover, Gerard, in her own home. The young man visits her disguised as a dancing-master and pretends to give her dancing-lessons. Hippolita is faced with a crisis when her father, Don Diego, an authoritarian old fool, decides to be present at the lessons. Since neither the young woman nor her lover know how to dance, Hippolita has to find a quick solution to prevent a disaster. She acts coy and tells her father that she is ashamed to show her clumsiness and ignorance.

Don Diego.   You must not be asham'd, Child, you'll never dance well, if you are asham'd.

Hippolita.   Indeed, I can't, Father, before you; 'tis my first lesson, and I shall do it so ill: pray, good Father, go into the next Room for this once, and the next time my Master comes, you shall see I shall be confident enough.

Don Diego.   Poor-foolish – innocent Creature; well, well, I will, Child, who but a Spanish kind of a Father cou'd have so innocent a Daughter?[7]

January and May relationships lend themselves also to misunderstandings. The old man who makes a fool of himself over a girl, and the middle-aged woman who desires a young lover are well-known comic characters. They are easily victimized, thanks to their blindness, by the young people who know their foibles. Even nice old ladies are prone

---

[7] William Wycherly, *The Gentleman Dancing-Master* in *The Complete Plays*, ed. and intro. Gerald Weales (New York: Doubleday, 1966), p. 165.

to be charmed and deceived by winsome young men, as is Lady Wood-
vil who, in Etherege's *The Man of Mode,* mistakes the rakish Dorimant
for a serious, sedate, and conservative young man.

In Restoration drama man's inability to understand his fellow beings
remains a secondary theme and does not become the major source of
amusement. Yet, human imperceptiveness still is part of nearly every
comedy. Each playwright creates his own brand of comic character
when he utilizes such misunderstandings. Shadwell, who likes to portray humor characters, makes his fools absurdly blind to others, whereas Congreve gives his silly-wise fools the opportunity to recognize at
least some people for what they are.

In Shadwell's *The Squire of Alsatia* the two major figures who are
incapable of knowing others are Belfond Senior and his father Sir William Belfond. The playwright reinforced their inherent ignorance by
suggesting that both have lived on their country-estates most of their
lives and therefore lack the sophistication of the city. When old Sir
William Belfond leaves for a six-week trip to Holland, the son takes
the opportunity to celebrate the occasion. He goes with his servant
Lolpoop on a secret holiday to London to have a good time and learn
the ways of the city.

In London, Belfond Senior is quickly singled out by a group of
crooks as a "bubble", a country squire who could be easily fleeced of
his inheritance. The three rogues who take him under their care are
Cheatly, a rascal who helps future heirs "to Goods Money upon great
disadvantage; is bound for them, and shares with them, till he undoes
them"; Shamwell, "cousin to the Belfonds, an heir, who being ruin'd
by Cheatly, is made a Decoy-Duck of others", and Captain Hackum,
a "Block-headed Bully" and a "cowardly, imprudent fellow".[8]

Belfond Senior is enchanted with their company and mistakes them
for noble, sophisticated gentlemen. To him they are "true and loving
friends", the "purest company" (p. 212) and the "prettiest Wits that are
in the Town" (p. 244). They are "very deep and sharp; sharp as Needles,
adad; the wittiest men in England", and they are "all of them stout as
Hector" (p. 246). The country squire finds Cheatly "very much a
gentleman" (p. 210) and believes about his "dear Friend Captain Hackum" that there is "no braver fellow under the Sun" (p. 244).

Shadwell emphasizes Belfond Senior's lack of perception when he

---

[8] Thomas Shadwell, *The Squire of Alsatia* in *The Complete Works of Thomas
Shadwell,* ed. Montague Summers (London: The Fortune Press, 1927), Vol. IV.
pp. 206-207. Further references to this play are given in text, by page-numbers.

compares him with his companion, the illiterate Lolpoop. The servant has more sense than his master despite the fact that he is only a simple country bumpkin. When Belfond Senior enthusiastically praises the crooks and calls them his loving and dear friends, Lolpoop profoundly remarks: "Ah! dear, loving Dogs! They love him by'r Lady, as a Cat loves a Mause" (p. 234). He tries to warn his master about the company he keeps: "Sir, Sir, let me speak one work with yeow; ods-flesh, I'll dye the Death of a Dog, and aw these yeow seen here, be not Rogues, Cheats and Pick-pockets'" (p. 215). Lolpoop is aware that Hackum, despite his boasts and menacing ways, is a coward. When the captain threatens to beat him, he answers him back: "Hawd you, hawd you: And I take kibbo, I'st raddle the Bones o' thee; Ise tell a that: for aw th'art a Captain mun" (p. 234). Belfond Senior scolds his servant and does not listen to his warning, and the rogues who are afraid of his sharp tongue find a buxom lady to keep Lolpoop occupied and quiet.

Eventually Belfond Senior is told by several people that he has fallen into the hands of crooks and is blatantly cheated by them. He does not believe anyone, not even his brother who tries every method of persuasion to make him see the truth. Even when Hackum is beaten up and led around the room by his nose the Country Squire still insists that "the Captain's a Lyon!" (p. 234). It takes a last-minute rescue from a marriage with a lady of questionable virtue and the arrest of the crooks to make Belfond Senior ask himself: "What are all these Rogues? and that a Whore? and am I cheated?" (p. 274). Despite Belfond Senior's realization that the crooks made a "Put, a Caravan, a Bubble" (p. 280) of him one is convinced that he will never be able to know any human being for what he is.

Sir William Belfond's lack of perception is also out of proportion, but it is more realistically portrayed than that of his son. He has an inflexible, dogmatic mind which prevents him from seeing others and which does not allow for the consideration of other peoples' views. His narrow interests limit his vision to his own little world. He is preoccupied with money matters and can not understand his brother, Sir Edward Belfond, who considers business affairs of secondary importance. Sir Edward on the other hand knows Sir William's nature and tells him: "Well, Brother, you are a happy man; for Wealth flows in upon you on every side, and Riches you account the greatest happiness" (p. 219). Sir William denies this but soon his avid interest in money is demonstrated. He is looking for a suitable bride for his son, Belfond Senior, and seems to be less interested in the girl's nature than in her dowry, which amounts to fifteen thousand pounds. Sir Edward wonders if the young woman, who is a puritan, would make a suitable wife for Belfond Senior.

Sir Edward.	The person of this Girl is well chosen for your son, if she were not so precise and pure.
Sir William.	Prethee, what matter what she is, has she not Fifteen Thousand Pounds clear?
Sir Edward.	For a Husband to differ in Religion from a Wife.
Sir William.	What, with Fifteen Thousand Pound?
Sir Edward.	A precise Wife will think her self so pure, she will be apt to condemn her Husband.
Sir William.	Ay, but Fifteen Thousand Pound, brother.
Sir Edward.	You know how intractable misguided Zeal and Spiritual Pride are.
Sir William.	What with Fifteen Thousand Pound!
Sir Edward.	I would not willingly my Son should have her.
Sir William.	Not with Fifteen Thousand Pound?
Sir Edward.	I see there's no Answer to be given to Fifteen Thousand Pound.

Sir Edward gives up in desperation after he realizes that his brother is only interested in money and does not care about his son's happiness.

Sir William also has decided theories about education. He lets his enlightened and liberal brother bring up his younger son, but of the education of Belfond Senior he takes care himself. Sir William's educational method is based on the motto: "Cudgel him, and allow him no money" (p. 220). He proudly tells Sir Edward about the result of his tutoring: "Well, I have a Son whom by my strictness I have form'd according to my heart: He never puts on his Hat in my presence; Rises at second Course, takes away his Plate, says Grace, and saves me Charge of a Chaplain. When ever he Committed a fault, I maul'd him with Correction: I'd fain see him once dare to be extravagant: No, he's a good Youth, the Comfort of my Age; I weep for joy to think of him" (p. 220).

By the time the young man grows up he "can handle Sheep or Bullock as well as any one: Knows his seasons of Plowing, Sowing, Harrowing, laying fallow: Understands all sorts of Manure: And ne're a one that wears a Head can wrong him in a Bargain" (p. 231). For the rest, Belfond Senior is ignorant because his father believes that Greek and Latin would teach him only to "prate like a Pedant" (p. 231), travel would make only an "arrant vain coxcomb" (p. 232) of him, and the rest of knowledge, like literature, history, mathematics and laws, are useless because he won't learn, "ever get a Six-pence, or improve his Estate by 'em" (p. 231).

Belfond Senior, according to his father, is a "solid Young Man, a Dutiful Child as ever man had" (p. 217) and he "knows no Vice poor Boy" (p. 231). When Sir William is informed that the young man has disappeared from the country estate he is deeply upset.

Sir William.	Oh my poor Boy! Robb'd and Murder'd and buried in some Ditch, or flung into some Pond. Oh, I shall never see thee more, dear Tim! The Joy, and the Support of all my Life! The only Comfort which I had on earth.
Sir Edward.	Have patience Brother; 'tis nothing but a little Ramble in your Absence.
Sir William.	Oh, no! he durst not Ramble; he was the dutifullest Child! I shall never see his face. . . . (p. 256)

When Sir William finds out that "one so strictly, so soberly Educated" (p. 256) indeed went on a "Ramble" and carouses with crooks in the most disreputable places, he is outraged and turns against his offspring. He calls him an "audacious Varlet", a "pernicious Wretch" (p. 263) and is ready to deny the inheritance to that "most ungracious Rebel, that Monster of Villainy" (p. 267).

Sir William does not know his younger son either. He believes that Belfond Junior, who was brought up by his brother Sir Edward and spent his youth studying and traveling, is a debauched rogue. Sir Edward loves the young man and believes that he is a decent fellow who will settle down to a worthwhile and productive life after his youthful escapades. Sir William rebukes him: "Your over-weening makes you look through a false glass upon him" (p. 219). But it is Sir William who looks through false glasses and has to learn that his younger son is not a libertine whose "Gentleman Education is come to Drinking, Whoring, and Debauchery" (p. 232), but a noble, helpful, "good natur'd Boy" (p. 272).

In *Love for Love* one also encounters an authoritarian father who looks at his sons through false glasses, but Congreve gives more flexibility and perception to his characters than Shadwell does.

Sir Sampson has some reason to be disappointed in his son, Valentine. The young man has squandered his money and lived a gay, irresponsible life. Sir Sampson feels that Valentine was a "good hopeful lad, till he learned to be a wit".[9] The old gentleman does not like wits

---

[9]   Congreve, *Love for Love* in *Complete Plays*, p. 272. Further references to this play are given in text, by page-numbers.

and is especially upset that his son does not heed his paternal warnings and commands. He complains to his friend Foresight: "What, I warrant my son thought nothing belonged to a father but forgiveness and affection, no authority, no correction, no arbitrary power; nothing to be done, but for him to offend, and me to pardon. I warrant you, if he danced till doomsday, he thought I was to pay the piper" (p. 272). Sir Sampson decides to be "revenged on his undutiful rogue" (p. 272), and disinherits Valentine in favor of the younger brother, Ben, who spent the last three years on the sea and is expected to return home to his family.

The irate father is not capable of seeing that Valentine is a generous and decent young man who, after he has fallen in love with the lovely Angelica, is ready to settle down and mend his ways. Sir Sampson maliciously misinterprets Valentine's actions, calls him an "unnatural whelp" (p. 237) and an "ill-natured dog" (p. 237) when the young man does not comply with his demands. The father who is a mercenary and hard man projects his own nature into Valentine when he accuses him of not having "a drachm of generous love about him" (p. 237), and being only interested in money and Angelica's estate.

Whereas Sir Sampson feels that Valentine is unlike him (p. 222) and therefore unacceptable, he welcomes enthusiastically his younger son and calls him "a chip of the old block" (p. 242). Ben, "an absolute sea-wit", is rather crude and his father soon has sense enough to notice this. He admits that this son needs some polishing but considers him still the "hopes of the family" (p. 236). Sir Sampson changes his opinion about Ben when the young man refuses to marry the girl his father has chosen for him. Ben relates with great relish the controversy with his father: "I told'n in plain terms, if I were minded to marry I'd marry to please myself, not him: and for the young woman that he provided for me, I thought it more fitting for her to learn her sampler and make dirt-pies, than to look after a husband" (pp. 259-260). Ben's comment enrages Sir Sampson and Ben remarks: "So he said he'd make my heart ache; and if so be that he could get a woman to his mind, he'd marry himself. Gad, says I, an you play the fool and marry at these years, there's more danger of your head aching than my heart. – He was woundy angry when I gav'n that wipe" (p. 260).

Shadwell exploits only the father and son controversy in his play but Congreve adds a new dimension to his portrait of a man who can't judge people and whose grey hairs "cover a green head" (p. 257). Sir Sampson decides to marry Angelica and in the last part of *Love for*

Love the comic possibilities of the January-May relationship are brought into play: Sir Sampson courts Angelica with youthful ardor. Ben, who is rather skeptical about his father's passion, warns him: "Mess, I fear his fire's little better than tinder; mayhap it will only serve to light a match for somebody else. The young woman's a handsome young woman, I can't deny it; but, father, if I might be your pilot in this case, you should not marry her. It's just the same thing, as if so be you sail so far as the Straits without provision" (p. 280). Sir Sampson is blind to Angelica's real nature and thinks at first that she is mercenary and that she would marry him for his money. Later he deludes himself by believing that the girl is actually in love with him.

Sir Sampson, not knowing the young people, is easily manipulated by them. He shows remarkable insight, though, when he encounters Angelica's uncle, Old Foresight. Foresight is inordinately superstitious and occupies himself with solving dreams, interpreting omens, and setting up horoscopes for himself and others. He is married to a young woman who, as everybody knows, deceives him. Foresight is jealous and suspects that his wife is interested in other men, but instead of facing up to the problem he consults the stars. Mrs. Foresight's horoscope indicates that, "She is young and sanguine, has a wanton hazel eye and was born under Gemini, which may incline her to society; she has a mole upon her lip, with a moist palm, and an open liberality on the mount of Venus" (p. 219). After interpreting the signs of her constellation and considering his own fortune – he was born "when the Crab was ascending" and therefore all his "affairs go backward" (p. 215) – Old Foresight comes to the conclusion: "Well – why, if I was born to be a cuckold there's no more to be said" (p. 219).

Sir Sampson knows Foresight, whose obsessions blind him to the world around him, and does his best to help him. He suggests that one does not learn about man's nature by reading and interpreting his horoscope: "If the sun shine by day, and the stars by night why, we shall know one another's faces without the help of a candle, and that's all the stars are good for" (p. 220). Foresight ends up as a cuckold and Sir Sampson is made a fool by Angelica whose keen perception of people enables her to remain aloof of all humiliating entanglements. She is inscrutable even to Valentine, who puzzles over her nature. He complains: "She is harder to be understood than a piece of Egyptian antiquity, or an Irish manuscript: you may pore till you spoil your eyes, and not improve your knowledge" (p. 269): Angelica loves, but without being blinded by the little Western flower. Though her heart had been touched by Cupid's dart her vision remains clear and keen, like that of the virgin huntress, Diana.

The dew of Dian's bud could never sharpen the vision of those who were born blind or those who bathed their eyes in the juice of the narcissus. Even in the realm of the ordinary, semi-aware beings, the knowledge of others is a rare gift. Shakespeare's young people and would-be actors wander around in the forest near Athens. They stumble in the darkness, catch occasional glimpses of each other by the pale moonlight only to lose each other and go astray again. Puck plays naughty tricks upon them, changing their vision and leading them on a merry chase. Invisible and hidden from human eyes he observes together with Oberon the pageantry of folly and remarks:

Lord, What fools these mortals be![10]

A COMPANY OF GAUDY NOTHINGS: MANNERS

Samuel Pepys' diary reflects his avid interest in the trivialities of his day: the current gossip about the theatre, the latest news about fashions and love-affairs. He seeks out people who are knowledgeable in these matters and mentions his pleasant afternoon visit with Willet's aunt, who understands "all the things of note touching plays and fashions and Court and everything",[11] and his dinner with the Pierce family which he enjoyed as it was "very good company and good discourse, they being able to tell me all the business of the Court; the amours and the mad doings that are there; how for certain Mrs. Stewart do everything with the king that a mistress should do; and that the king hath many bastard children that are known and owned, besides the Duke of Monmouth" (p. 186).

Pepys gathers all the gossip about public figures among which the King's mistress, Mrs. Castlemaine, is his favorite. After one of his strolls in the Whitehall garden he reports: "... in the Privygarden saw the finest smocks and linnen petticoats of my Lady Castlemayne's, laced with rich lace at the bottom, that ever I saw; and did me good to look upon them" (p. 66). He watches her at the theatre and makes a note one evening in his diary: "One thing of familiarity I observed in

---

[10] Shakespeare, III.2., 115.
[11] Samuel Pepys, *Samuel Pepys Diary*, ed. Richard LeGallienne (New York: The Modern Library, Random House, 1956), p. 258. Further references to this work are given in text, by page-numbers.

my Lady Castlemayne: she called to one of her women . . . for a little patch off her face, and put it into her mouth and wetted it, and so clapped it upon her own by the side of her mouth, I suppose she feeling a pimple rising there" (p. 292).

Beauty-patches, wigs, dresses, feathers, all fashionable costumes fascinate Pepys. He takes walks in the park so he can see the queen dressed for her outing and eagerly watches the courtiers and their ladies at the ball. He reports the great news: "The King hath yesterday in council declared his resolution of setting a fashion for clothes, which he will never alter. It will be a vest, I know not well how" (p. 292). A week later Pepys mentions seeing the King and some of his followers dressed in the new garment which is a "long cassocke close to the body, of black cloth, and pinked with silke under it, and a coat over it, and the legs ruffled with black riband like pigeon's leg; and, upon the whole, I wish the king may keep it, for it is a very fine and handsome garment" (p. 209).

Pepys himself is a dandy who likes to order and wear fashionable clothes. He mentions with great satisfaction: "This day I first put on my slasht doublet, which I like very well." Another time he expects impatiently a newly ordered suit and when it does not arrive puts on the "late new black silke camelott suit" (p. 164). The new finery arrives just when he has finished dressing, "when fully ready comes my new coloured ferrandin, which my wife puts me out of love with which vexes me, but I think it is only my not being used to wear colours which makes it look a little unusual upon me" (p. 164).

Pepys likes to dress according to the latest fashion and engage in the activities of high society. He hires a dancing-master to teach him and his wife the latest dances. First he is reluctant to pay ten shillings for a lesson but then consoles himself with: "The truth is, I think it a thing very useful for a gentleman, and sometimes I may have occasion of using it" (p. 97). Pepys also uses more and more French words in his diary as time passes, as it is the fashionable language used by the King and the gallants. He often employs the language to record his indiscretions with various ladies. "I did give the pretty maid Betty that comes to me half-a-crown for coming and had a *baiser* or two – *elle* being mighty *jolie*", writes the amorous philanderer.

Pepys could easily have become one of the successful comic characters in Restoration drama which abounds in wonderful caricatures of fops, gallants, beaux, and coxcombs, whose main concern is to imitate the great and be received by the fashionable world. Though Shad-

well himself portrays such personages, he asserts in one of his pessi-
mistic moods that manners characters mainly amuse those who like
cheap entertainment.

> The rabble of little People, are most pleas'd with Jack Puddings being
> soundly kick'd, or having a Custard handsomely thrown in his face, than
> with all the wit in Plays: and the higher sort of Rabble (as there may be a
> rabble of very fine people in this illiterate age) are more pleased with the
> extravagant and unnatural actions, the trifles, and fripperies of a Play or
> the trappings and ornaments of Nonsense, than with all the wit in the world.
> This is one reason why we put our Fops into extravagant, and unnatural
> habits; it being a Cheap way of conforming to the understanding of those
> brisk, gay Sparks, that judge of Wit or Folly by the Habit; that being
> indeed the only measure they can take in judging of Mankind, who are
> Criticks in nothing but a Dress.[12]

Shadwell's misanthropic character Stanford echoes the sentiments of
his creator. When his friend Lovel advises him to enjoy himself, to
attend the gay performances in the theatre, to meet relations and good
friends, the morose young man responds only with complaints: all
these pleasures are vulgar, futile or boring. Then Lovel advises him:

Lovel.   ...then change the Scene, and Go to Court, where Conver-
             sation is refin'd.
Stanford.   Why so I do; but there I find a company of gaudy nothings.
             That fain would be Courtiers.[13]

Most of the Restoration dramatists and their characters are more
positively inclined than Shadwell is. The authors themselves belong to
the court and the fashionable set and enjoy watching the gatherings
of gaudy nothings. They incorporate them in their plays, not only for
amusement of the higher sort of rabble, but for those who are fair
judges of wit and folly. The unsuccessful mimics of fashion and the
affected snobs whose pretentions are seen through are especially appreciated in the seventeenth century. It is an age which has an ample
share of gilded butterflies, men who try (but do not always succeed) in
living up to the elaborate social code of the brilliant courts of England
and France.

Many of the gaudy nothings are preoccupied with that which is new
and currently fashionable. Olivia, from Wycherly's *The Plain Dealer*,
describes her admirer Novel before she lets him join her company: he

---

[12] Shadwell, Preface to *The Humorists* in *The Complete Works of Thomas Shadwell*, p. 185.
[13] Shadwell, *The Sullen Lovers* in *The Complete Works of Thomas Shadwell*,
Vol. I, p. 20.

is a coxcomb who "affects Novelty as much as the Fashion, and is as fantastical as changeable, as well known as the Fashion; who likes nothing but what is new." [14] Wycherly's Sir Simon Addleplot would like to use the currently fashionable words but he admits that he has had no luck in doing so. Farquhar's Mockmode, "a young Squire come newly from the University, and setting up for a Beau", [15] and his servant Club are also eager to learn the newest fads. Mockmode, who takes lessons from Rigadoon the dancing-master, confides in his mentor: "Cou'd I but dance well, push well, play upon the Flute, and swear the most fashionable Oaths, I wou'd set up for Quality with e're a young Nobleman of 'em all. – Pray what are the most fashionable Oaths in Town? Zoons, I take it, is a very becoming one." [16] Ridagoon corrects his pupil: "Zoons is only us'd by the disbanded Officers and Bullies: but Zauns is the Beaux pronunciation." [17] Mockmode thus learns to say Zauns and also to "take Snush, Grin, and make an humble Cringe". [18]

Brisk, one of Shadwell's fops, is not so much concerned with the proper language as with fashionable appearance. He believes that he has excellent taste and gives free instructions about color schemes and clothes to his friend Drybob.

Brisk.   Here's a Perriwig, no Flax in the world can be whiter; how
            delicately it appears by this colour'd Hanging, and let me advise
            you ever while you live, if you have a fair Peruke, get by a
            Green or some dark colour'd Hanging or Curtain, if there be
            one in the Room. Oh, it sets it off admirably.
Drybob.   A very Metaphysical Notion.
Brisk.   And be sure if your Eye brows not black, to black 'em soundly;
            ah your Black Eye-brow is your fashionable Eye-brow. I hate
            Rogues that wear Eye-brows that are out of fashion. [19]

Brisk is also proud of his clothes and believes that the ladies flock around him because he wears extraordinary, fancy suits. "I always love to do things en Cavalier", [20] says Brisk and explains how he at times catches the attention of his lady-friends: "Look you, no Man appears better upon a Bench in the Playhouse, when I stand up to expose my

[14] Wycherly, *The Complete Plays*, p. 412.
[15] George Farquhar, *Love and a Bottle* in *The Complete Works of George Farquhar*, Vol. I, p. 10.
[16] *Love and a Bottle*, p. 25.
[17] *Ibid.*
[18] *Love and a Bottle*, p. 26.
[19] Shadwell, *The Humorists*, p. 221.
[20] *The Humorists*, p. 223.

Person between the Acts; I take out my Comb, and with a *bonne mien* comb my Periwig to the Tune the Fiddles play." [21]

Wycherly's sober Manly does "weigh the man, not his title",[22] but many of the gallants are snobs and name-droppers. Sparkish the fop just has to tell his companions that he is going to dine with an Earl at Whitehall. His friend Dorilant acidly remarks: "Why I thought thou hadst lov'd a Man with a title better, than a Suit with a French trimming to't." [23] Though Sparkish assures him that this is not at all true, he soon intimates that he has access to the King's chambers and is even at times present when his highness dines. Congreve's Tattle is also a snob who likes his friends to believe that he has had numerous affairs with titled ladies. When they press him to reveal their names, he becomes suddenly rather vague and secretive.

A Gentleman not only knows the right people but has also traveled and seen the world. At least he has visited France and knows the latest fads and fashions. On rare occasions one encounters characters whose visit to another country turns out to be an enriching and beneficial experience as in the case of Farquhar's Harry Wildair, a "Spark just come from France / But then so far from Beau – why he talks sense!" [24] Throughout *The Constant Couple* one discerns Farquhar's attitude toward those who travel: when a sensible man visits another country he returns enlightened and enriched by the experience, but when a fool travels the results are diastrous. Clincher Junior, the country-bumpkin, intends to take a trip to France and is discouraged by Colonel Standard: "The Travel of such Fools as you doubly Injures our Country, you expose our Native Follies, which Ridicules us amongst Strangers, and return fraught only with Vices which you vend here for Fashionable Gallantry; a Traveling Fool is as dangerous as a Homebred Villain." [25] Colonel Standard is frank and so is Dryden's Doralice when she tells a gallant newly arrived from France: "You travelling monsieurs live upon the stock you have got abroad . . . When you have regorged what you have taken in, you are the leanest things in Nature." [26] The dunces learn the wrong things wherever they are and their

---

[21] *The Humorists*, p. 244.
[22] Wycherly, *The Plain Dealer*, p. 394.
[23] Wycherly, *The Country Wife* in *The Complete Plays*, p. 278.
[24] Farquhar, *The Constant Couple om The Complete Works of George Farpuhar* p. 87.
[25] *The Constant Couple*, p. 244.
[26] John Dryden, *Marriage a la Mode* in *Three Plays*, ed. George Saintsbury (New York: Hill and Wang, 1958), p. 186.

experience instead of improving them manages to illuminate their shortcomings. Restoration writers not only ridicule the would-be-sophistication of these fools but also censor the ridiculous French customs which replace sensible native ways.

Sir Car Scroope, who wrote the prologue to *Sir Fopling Flutter*, sums up the attitude of most playwrights of his age when he says: "Of foreign wares why should we fetch the scum When we can be so richly served at home." [27] Many authors ridicule those who unsuccessfully imitate foreign customs. Some of the best known comic characters who combine their "native follies" with those learned from other nations are Dryden's Melantha; Wycherly's fools, Monsieur de Paris and Don Diego; and Etherege's famous gallant, Sir Fopling Flutter.

Dryden's Melantha is blindly taken in by everything that is French. "No lady can be so curious of a new fashion, as she of a new French word: she's the very mint of the nation; and as fast as any bullion comes out of France, coins it immediately into our language." [28] The other outstanding trait that characterizes the young woman is her predominant and "insufferable humour of haunting the court" (pp. 190-191). She is a snob who wants to be part of the court-life and be accepted by the King and the Queen. Melantha thus occupies her time by annoying the royal family and studying French. Every day she learns new words from her French maid Philotis and liberally sprinkles her conversation with them. Melantha flirts with Rodolphe, a young man who courts her though he is married to Doralice. She approves of him because "he's a fine man, he signs and dances *en Français*, and writes the *billet-doux* to a miracle" (p. 198). Doralice has a less complimentary view of her husband and the French generally. She tells Rodolphe: "You are an admirer of the dull French poetry, which is so thin, that it is the very leaf-gold of wit, the very wafers and whipped cream of sense, for which a man opens his mouth, and gapes, to swallow nothing; and to be an admirer of such profound dullness, one must be endowed with a great perfection of impudence and ignorance" (p. 242).

When Rodolphe's friend Palamede meets Melantha for the first time he is amused at her affectations. She is only interested in him because he came recently to the town and she wants to know about the newest

---

[27] Sir George Etherege, Prologue to *Sir Fopling Flutter* in *Plays and Poems*, ed. and intro. A. Wilson Verity (London: John C. Nimmo, 1888), p. 241.
[28] Dryden, *Marriage a la Mode*, p. 190. Further references to this play are given in text, by page-numbers.

French fashions, the latest minuet and "who danced best in the last grand-ballet" (p. 200). Though the young woman is foolish, she is also very pretty and Palamede wonders how he'll be able to win her love. He is helped by Melantha's French maid who knows her mistress and enlightens the young man about her habits and nature: "Be sure only to ply her with French words, and I'll warrant you'll do business. Here are a list of phrases for this day: use them to her upon all occasions, and foil her at her own weapon; for she's like one of the old Amazons, she'll never marry, except it be the man who has first conquered her (p. 250).

Palamede, following Philotis' advice, when he next meets Melantha outdoes her in her affectations. Melantha first becomes angry and complains: "He mocks himself on me, he abuses me" (p. 252), then she cries and at last she perceives her own ridiculousness and laughs. The two young people eventually fall in love. Melantha consents to marry Palamede but, like Millamant, she wants to dictate certain conditions before she weds him. Palamede objects: "No; I will hear no conditions! I am resolved to win you *en Français:* to be very airy, with abundance of noise, and no sense" (p. 253).

Melantha is never completely cured of her folly. Palamede is well aware that, though she is lovely and charming, she will always remain a snob. He knows that if they are going to marry, he will have to cater to her whims. Thus he sensibly plans for the future: "I find I must get her a place at court; for she is young enough, and pretty enough, to bring up a fashion there to be affected" (p. 262).

Melantha, a silly-wise, delightful girl, is the sole "manners" character in a comedy which deals mainly with the question of noble and heroic love contrasted with more common and everyday affection. In Wycherly's *The Gentleman Dancing-Master* the theme itself deals with the question of manners and affectations.

Hippolita, the daughter of an English merchant who has lived fifteen years in Spain and considers himself a Spaniard, is engaged to her cousin Monsieur de Paris. The young man, who spent three months in France, mainly in the company of coachmen and lackeys, affects the customs of that country and fancies himself to be a sophisticated French gallant. Hippolita eventually meets Gerard who according to Monsieur de Paris "has been abroad as much as many man, and does not make the least show of it, but a little in his Meen, not at all in his discour Jernie; he never talks so much as of *St. Peters* Church, and *Rome,* the Escurial, or *Madrid,* nay not so much as of *Henry IV,* of

Pont-Neuf, Paris, and the new *Louvre,* nor of the *Grand Roy.*"[29]

The sensible Hippolita is attracted to Gerard who eventually gains access to her in the guise of a dancing-master. After he outwits his rival, Monsieur, and the father, Don Diego, he marries Hippolita. The two lovers are aware that it is foolish to ape foreign customs but the two fools aren't. Nathaniel Parris, son of a beer-brewer, calls himself Monsieur de Paris. He is amused at his future father-in-law's pretentions but does not perceive his own follies. The same is true of old James Formal, alias Don Diego, who finds Monsieur very funny, but who never realizes that he is as ridiculous as the frenchified fop.

Monsieur has preconceived ideas about the characteristics of a typical Frenchman and he avidly conforms with his own absurd precepts. He believes that Frenchmen love to joke, are never jealous, and pepper their speeches with oaths. When Gerard tells him that they are also slovenly he wonders at first.

Monsieur.	Slovenly! you mean negligent?
Gerard.	No, I mean slovenly.
Monsieur.	Then I will be more slovenly.
Gerard.	You know, to be a perfect French-man, you must never be silent, never sit still, and never be clean. (p. 144)

Because he considers Gerard an expert in such matters, Monsieur takes the advice to heart.

He, like other fools, mistakes "the contempt and scorn of people for applause and admiration" (p. 171) and takes Gerard's following remarks as raillery: "Monsieur, now give me leave to admire thee, that in three months at Paris you could renounce your Language, Drinking and your Country ... and come home so perfect a *French*-man, that the Drey-men of your Fathers own Brew-house wou'd be ready to knock thee in the head" (p. 143). Monsieur indeed has renounced his native language and is proud that he is speaking "agreeable ill *Englis*" (p. 143) because " 'tis as ill breeding now to speak good *Englis*' as to write good *Englis*', good sense or a good hand" (p. 143). Monsieur is gratified when others laugh at his expense. He tells his fiance, "you see wat it is to have been in France; before I went into France I cou'd get no body to laugh at me, ma foy" (p. 171). He tells her that "to play the Fool is the Science in France", and that many cavaliers go over "to learn to be the Buffoon; but for all dat, dey return but *mauvais* Buf-

---

[29] Wycherly, *The Gentleman Dancing-Master*, p. 134. Further references to this play are given in text, by page-numbers.

foon (p. 171). Hippolita assures him that he did exceptionally well and managed to become "the greatest Fool in England" (p. 172).

Hippolita's father is the second greatest fool in England. Though he speaks good English he sprinkles his sentences with Spanish oaths, wears a Spanish outfit, and lives according to Spanish maxims and proverbs. He knows what a proper Spaniard should be and behaves accordingly: "I am as grave, grum, and jealous, as any Spaniard breathing" (p. 152). He has no intention to be English and insists: "I will be a Spaniard in every thing still, and will not conform, not I, to their ill-favor'd English Customs, for I will wear my Spanish Habit still, I will stroke by Spanish Whiskers still, and I will eat my Spanish Olio still" (p. 152).

Everybody enjoys the clash between the two fools, including the irreverent Hippolita who observes with amusement the "sport . . . betwixt these two Contraries" (p. 174). Both gentlemen find each others' clothes outrageously funny. Don Diego finds Monsieur's outfit "wonderfully ridiculous" and calls him "Monsieur de Pantalloons" (p. 175). He tells him that his pants make him "look and waddle (with all those gew-gaw Ribbons) like a great old Fat, slovenly waterdog" (p. 176). Monsieur is equally delighted with Don Diego's appearance. He retorts: ". . . your Spanish Hose, and your Nose in the Air, make you look a grisled-long-Irish-Greyhound, reaching a Crust off from a high Shelf, ha, ha, ha" (p. 176). Don Diego has the last word though. He compels Monsieur to change his ways by telling him that he can't marry Hippolita unless he speaks good English and dresses in Spanish clothes.

Hippolita warns her father that " 'tis hard for him to cease being Monsieur, as 'tis for you to break a Spanish Oath" (p. 191), but Don Diego insists on the change. Monsieur very reluctantly sheds piece by piece his French outfit and dons instead Spanish clothes. The metamorphosis does not improve him and Don Diego has enough sense to remark: "Well, the Hood does not make the Monk, the Ass was an Ass still, though he had the Lyons Skin on; this will be a light French Fool, in spite of the Grave Spanish Habit, look you" (p. 194).

Don Diego's unwillingness to change is as ridiculous as Monsieur's seeming willingness to learn. Both are riddled with obsessions, concerned with trivialities and attired in their folly: one in the stiff Spanish collar and formal, somber habit, the other covered with nonsensical ribbons and silly fripperies. Both are clownish, yet not entirely mechanical characters as Wycherly endows them with traits which give them life and a certain amount of flexibility. Monsieur has a moment of insight when he catches a glimpse of his own absurdity and Don Diego, despite his rigid behavior, is capable of genuine and warm affection for his daughter.

Etherege's great comic creation Sir Fopling Flutter is also an artificial character who has some redeeming traits. He has not much insight or even feelings but he is well brought up and educated. He is an absurd coxcomb dressed in fancy clothes yet, as Dryden says, in the epilogue to *The Man of Mode:* "Sir Fopling is a fool so nicely writ, / The ladies would mistake him for a wit." [30] Though Sir Fopling is more sophisticated than Monsieur de Paris, he is still only an imitator who apes for better or worse other people and other customs.

> He's knight o' th' shire, and represents ye all.
> From each he meets he culls whate'er he can,
> Legion's his name, a people in a man:
> His bulky folly gathers as it goes,
> And, rolling o'er you, like a snowball grows. (p. 374)

Sir Fopling is vain and conceited. He "thinks himself the pattern of modern gallantry" (p. 256), an accomplished gentleman who should be appreciated by all. His friend Bellair reports that on one of his visits to a lady he gave her "a catalogue of his good qualities under the character of a complete gentleman, who, according to Sir Fopling, ought to dress well, dance well, fence well, have a genius for love-letters, an agreeable voice for a chamber, be very amorous, something discreet, but not over-constant". (p. 257). Although Sir Fopling has a high opinion of his own qualities, others know him to be "a person of great acquired follies" (p. 257), one whom traveling has managed to make a more "eminent coxcomb" than he was before (p. 257). He is a "caravan lately arrived from Paris" (p. 309) dressed in the most fashionable and fancy French clothes.

One of the gallants who catches a glimpse of Sir Fopling Flutter in the theatre reports that "he was yesterday at the play, with a pair of gloves up to his elbows and a periwig more exactly curled than a lady's head newly dressed for a ball" (p. 357). When the vain beau enters a room he immediately looks for a mirror so he can admire his appearance. His favorite conversation topic is the latest fashion in clothes. He chats with the ladies about their laces and discusses with them the difference between the "*point d'Espagne*" and the "*point de Venise*" (p. 296). He models his latest outfit for the company and calls their

---

[30]   Dryden, Epilogue to Etherege, *The Man of Mode*, p. 373. Further references to *The Man of Mode* are given in text, by page-numbers.

attention to the tassels, the long-waisted coat, the "pantaloons" (p. 297), and the fringed gloves. Sir Fopling wears only Paris originals and when the ladies wonder where he bought all the fancy clothes he proudly names the houses where he purchased his outfit.

Lady Townley.	The suit?
Sir Fopling.	Barroy.
Emilia.	The garniture?
Sir Fopling.	Le Gras.
Medley.	The shoes?
Sir Fopling.	Piccat.
Dorimant.	The wig?
Sir Fopling.	Chedreux.
Lady Townley and Emily.	The gloves?
Sir Fopling.	Orangerie: you know the smell ladies. (p. 298)

Sir Fopling likes exclusive clothes and loves exclusive people. His name-dropping is rather discreet. On one occasion he turns with compliments to Dorimant telling him, "I knew a French count so like thee" (p. 296). Another time he casually mentions: "I was well received in a dozen families where all the women of quality used to visit, I have intrigues to tell thee more pleasant than ever thou read'st in a novel" (p. 324). Sir Fopling is less subtle when he tells the whole company that he has just come from Whitehall "after the King's *couchee*", suggesting that he is on familiar terms with the royal family.

Like Pepys, who prides himself on knowing not only the right people but also the proper social graces, Sir Fopling is aware that in a sophisticated society one ought to be a connoisseur of music and dance. He attempts to surprise his friends by appearing disguised and bringing with him a group of "*balladins*" with "*flutes douces*" who'll perform for the audience the latest French music. Sir Fopling is recognized by all despite his mask, and when the ladies wonder if he can dance to the music Dorimant enlightens them: "He has no more excellence in his heels than his head. He went to Paris a plain bashful English blockhead, and is returned a fine undertaking French fop" (p. 327). Sir Fopling pretends to be too tired to dance and to avoid making a complete fool of himself excuses himself from singing to the music by stating that he has a too "weak voice" (p. 338).

Sir Fopling, Monsieur, and the other manners characters are eager to be approved by the rest of the world and especially by the social clique they find desirable. They are vain and are mainly preoccupied with trivialities. Their lives are filled with concern for that which is momentary, ephemeral, and of little value. Some, like Sir Fopling Flutter, pursue their interests with more flair and taste than do boobies like Monsieur. The latter fraternizes with coachmen and lackeys during his stay in Paris whereas the man of mode frequents the fashionable salons. The source of their information influences their behavior and also their ability to understand and assimilate new ways.

Dryden, who describes Sir Fopling as one who "culls what'ever he can" from everybody he encounters, suggests that the gallant has little personality of his own. He borrows his manners, knowledge, values and even the style of his clothes from somebody else and often fails by making the wrong choices or inadequately copying the original. Sir Fopling has to be just a bit more fashionable, more French, and more original than anybody else. Monsieur is at a disadvantage to begin with because he imitates the wrong people and has not enough sense to know the difference between elegance and vulgarity. Etherege's Loveit observes the fantastical Sir Fopling and asks: "Is there a thing so hateful as a senseless mimic?" (p. 347). She defines the unsuccessful imitator as a "ridiculous animal who has more of the ape than the ape has of the man in him" (p. 347).

The "senseless mimic" is mercilessly ridiculed in the world of the theatre where good imitation is essential. The bad actor who misunderstands his role or is not able to adapt himself to it is ostracized and so is the man who fails on the great stage of society. The ever shifting comedy of manners which changes from place to place and age to age requires agile and perceptive minds. The greatest ones conceive the roles and make the fashions as Charles the Second does. Smaller ones, like Pepys, observe carefully and attempt to copy the elite as accurately as they can. Monsieur and the others, who are neither capable of instituting new ways nor imitating them adequately, fail and become the fools and clowns of drama and society.

BELLOWS OF ZEAL: MORALS

In the Dedication of *The Double Dealer* to Charles Montague, Congreve answers his critics and defends his dramatic practices. He is especially concerned about the ladies who accuse him of representing some female characters as "vicious and affected".[31] Congreve first

---

[31]   Congreve, Dedication to *The Double Dealer*, p. 118.

gallantly states: "I would rather disoblige all the critics in the world than one of the fair sex", but he then proceeds to vindicate his ways and point out the dramatist's task: "It is the business of a comic poet to paint the vices and follies of humankind; and there are but two sexes, male and female, men and women, which have a title to humanity: and if I leave one half of them out, the work will be imperfect."[32]

Shadwell discusses in even greater detail the task and aims of the comic poet:

I confess, a Poet ought to do all that he can, decently to please, that so he may instruct. To adorn his Images of Vertue so delightfully to affect people with secret veneration of it in others, and an emulation to practice it in themselves: And to render their Figures of Vice and Folly so ugly and detestable, to make People hate and despise them, not only in others, but (if it be possible) in their dear selves. And in this latter, I think Comedy more useful than Tragedy; because the Vices and Follies in Courts (as they are too tender to be touch'd) so they concern but a few; whereas the Cheats, Villanies, and troublesome follies, in the common conversation of the world, are of concernments to all the Body of Mankind.[83]

Although, according to both authors, the comic poet should portray vice for the edification of the audience, this happens not too frequently in Restoration drama. Many of the comedies deal with the not too troublesome follies of mankind though a few do expose the darker side of life.

Restoration writers are aware that evil exists. They depict greedy fortune-hunters who plot to marry rich heiresses, younger brothers who wish their older brothers, who inherit the money, dead, and small-time crooks who enjoy fleecing their victims. Most of the true-wits in the comedies are aware that this is not the best of all possible worlds. Congreve's Scandal is keenly aware that the universe is populated with imperfect people. He is an expert on the subject as he is rather amoral himself. He argues at one point that prolonged pretentions eventually become truth and that there is "no effectual difference between continued affectation and reality".[34] Scandal insists that he sees people in their "true colours".[35] To illustrate he first describes some of his monster-acquaintances, "a lawyer with a hundred hands, two heads, and but one face, a divine with two faces, and one head, and . . . a soldier with his brains in his belly, and his heart where his head should

[32] *Ibid.*
[33] Shadwell, *The Humorists*, p. 184.
[34] Congreve, *Love for Love*, p. 232.
[35] *Love for Love*, p. 214.

be".[36] Scandal's unsavory gallery also includes two hypocrites, a society lady and a well-known gallant. He describes them with great relish: "I can show you pride, folly, affectation, wantonness, inconstancy, covetousness, dissimulation, malice, and ignorance, all in one piece. Then I can show you lying, foppery, vanity, cowardice, bragging, lechery, impotence, and ugliness in another piece; and yet one of these is a celebrated beauty, and t'other a professed beau."[37]

Scandal himself is a disreputable, but rather delightful, rake. When he attempts to seduce the pretty Mrs. Foresight, he encounters some difficulties. The young woman believes in virtue and is unwilling to give in to his advances. Though Scandal says that he too believes in virtue, he quickly qualifies his statement:

Scandal.   Yes, faith; I believe some women are virtuous too; but 'tis as I believe some men are valiant, through fear.
Mrs. Foresight. O monstrous! What are conscience and Honor?
Scandal.   Why: honour of a public enemy; and conscience a domestic thief, and he that would secure his pleasure, must pay a tribute to one, and go halves with t'other: As for honour, that you have secured; for you have purchased a perpetual opportunity for pleasure.
Mrs. Foresight. An opportunity for pleasure?
Scandal.   Ay, your husband; a husband is an opportunity for pleasure; so you have taken care of honour, and 'tis the least I can do to take care of conscience.
Mrs. Foresight. And so you think we are free for one another.[38]

Although Mrs. Foresight accuses Scandal of being a villainous character" and a "libertine in speech as well as in practice", she eventually lets herself be convinced by the young man.

Scandal's redeeming qualities are his wit and his charm. Like many of the Restoration rakes he knows the nature of immorality and vice, but seems to be convinced that it is more pleasurable to follow the wide path and leave the narrow one for others. He usually achieves what he desires and, thanks to his intelligence, escapes the chastisement of laughter.

Those who are ignorant of morals and even take delight in corruption are laughted at, but in a way they are also approved of. Mrs. Pinchwife, who learns to lie, cheat, and eventually to commit adultery without realizing that she is sinning, is the comic heroine of Wycherly's

---

[36] *Ibid.*
[37] *Ibid.*
[38] *Love for Love*, p. 247.

The Country Wife. Congreve's Prue is tutored by Tattle in the arts of fibbing and also in the pleasures of the bed. Her frank delight in the forbidden games and open approval of that which is usually concealed by others is amusing and rather charming.

The ones who become the butts of contemptuous laughter in Restoration comedy belong to the group of the partially aware. They are the hypocrites whose pretentions to goodness, virtue, honor, and saintliness are discovered. Fujimura in his book *The Restoration Comedy of Wit* points out that "the Wits of the Restoration attacked what they considered dogmatic and false: they criticized what they thought the pretenses of religion and morality, and they warred against what they believed to be hypocritical and unnatural." [39] The true-wits, some of them rakes like Dorimant, Horner, and Scandal, are not necessarily virtuous themselves. They often misbehave either openly or without being discovered and seldom are punished for their misdeeds. Many of them fit the description of Etherege's Wheedle who is "of a ready wit, pleasant conversation, thoroughly skilled in men; in a word, he knows so much virtue as makes him well accomplished for all manner of vice". [40] Congreve's Maskwell expresses the attitude of the rake who likes his crimes well executed. He pretends to be virtuous in a convincing way and proudly admirs, "I have the same face, the same words and accents, when I speak what I do think, and when I speak what I do not think – the very same – and dear dissimulation is the only art not to be known from nature." [41] The wits recognize the less artful hypocrites whose dissimulation is unsuccessful and who expose their weakness to the world. Though men come most frequently under attack, women, as Congreve indicates, also get their share of criticism.

The religious hypocrites who hide their greed and lust under the cover of seeming holiness are most frequently men. One encounters caricatures of puritans in Restoration comedy though they are not as well drawn as Ben Jonson's Tribulation Wholesome, Ananias, and Zeal-of-the-Land Busy. Sometimes they are only mentioned or they make a brief appearance on the stage as Smirk does. He is the chaplain of Lady Biggot who keeps him because he "will serve the flesh as well as the spirit". [42] The more extensively developed comic character do not

[39] Thomas H. Fujimura, *The Restoration Comedy of Wit* (Princeton: Princeton University Press, 1952), p. 70.
[40] Etherege, *Love in a Tub* in *Plays and Poems*, pp. 14-15.
[41] Congreve, *The Double Dealer*, p. 141.
[42] Etherege, *Sir Fopling Flutter*, p. 363.

belong to the clergy, but are usually older, middle-class citizens who pursue forbidden pleasures under the guise of saintliness.

In Farquhar's *The Constant Couple,* hypocrisy seems to be a family trait. Smuggler, the uncle, and Vizard, the nephew, are arrant pretenders. Each one has his own style and method. Smuggler is an old, lecherous merchant who "prays all Sunday for the sins of the Week past",[43] but who is inordinately greedy. "Hell hungers not more for wretched souls, then he for ill-got Pelf – and yet (what's wonderful) he that wou'd stick at no profiable Villainy himself, loves Holiness in another" (p. 137). Old Smuggler is especially fond of virtuous young women and so is his nephew Vizard, who in many ways resembles his uncle. He is "outwardly pious, otherwise a great Debauchee, and villanous" (p. 91). When the witty and gay Sir Harry Wildair encounters Vizard dressed as a gallant, he remarks: "I thought thy Hypocrisy had been wedded to Pulpit Cushion long ago" (p. 96). The young man is not at all surprised to hear such a comment for he is rather proud that he is an accomplished and imaginative pretender.

The unmasking of the uncle and the nephew is contrived by the comely Mistress Lurewell, who, as her name indicates, has many attractions. When alderman Smuggler visits Lurewell and attempts to cheat her out of her money, the young woman threatens to expose him and ruin his reputation. The old man is not at all impressed.

Smuggler.   Blast my Reputation! he, he, he,: why I'm a Religious Man, Madam, I have been very instrumental in the Reformation of Manners, ruin my Credit! ah, poor Woman! There is but one way Madam, – you have a sweet leering Eye.
Lurewell.   You instrumental in the Reformation! how?
Smuggler.   I whipt all the Whores, Cut and Long-Tail, out of the Parish – Ah! that leering Eye! Then I voted for putting down the playhouse – Ah that Ogle, that Ogle! – then my own pious Example – Ah that Lip, that Lip. (p. 111)

Mistress Lurewell knows that Smuggler is a hypocrite and a "Religious Rogue", and decides to "beat the old Monster" (p. 111). Smuggler, after appraising Lurewell's physical attractions, is eager to do "business" with her and demonstrates how he wishes to conduct the affair.

Smuggler.   See here, Madam, (Puts a piece of Money in his Mouth) Buss and Guinea, buss and Guinea, buss and Guinea. (p. 112)

Lurewell pretends to be amenable to his offer but asks him to return

---

[43]   Farquhar, *The Constant Couple,* p. 137. Further references to this play are given in text, by page-numbers.

disguised in the evening, "to secure both of our Honours" (p. 112). To the alderman this seems rather a superfluous precaution and throwing aside all pretense to virtue he freely admits: "P'shaw! no matter, I am an old Fornicator, I'm not half so Religious as I seem to be. You little Rogue, why I'm disguis'd as I am, our sanctity is all outside, all Hypocrisy" (p. 112).

Lurewell is also approached by the nephew, Vizard, who believes himself to be a paragon of discretion. He assures his lady-acquaintances that "like a Mole in the Earth, I dig deep but invisible, not like those fluttering noisie Sinners whose Pleasure is the proclamation of their Faults" (p. 136). Although Vizard does not consider himself to be a "noisie sinner" he loves to hear his own voice. He has a bad habit which eventually leads to his downfall: he enjoys soliloquizing about his vices and delivers his dramatic monologues in empty rooms.

Vizard, who also tries to win Lurewell's favors, is invited by her to an evening *rendez-vous*. The young man is unaware that he is scheduled to arrive at her house simultaneously with his uncle. At the appointed hour Smuggler appears at Mistress Lurewell's lodgings disguised as a woman. Immediately after his arrival someone else knocks on the door and the alderman quickly hides in a closet. Vizard enters and recites his dramatic soliloquy in the seemingly empty room.

Vizard.   Propitious Darkness guides the Lovers Steps, and Night that shadows outward sense, lights up our inward Joy. Night! the great awful Ruler of Mankind, which like the Persian Monrach, hides its Royalty to raise the Veneration of the World. Under thy easie Reign Dissemblers may speak Truth; all slavish Forms and Ceremonies laid aside, and generous Villainy may act without Constraint.
Smuggler.   (peeping out of the closet) Bless me! What Voice is this?
Vizard.   Our hungry appetites like the wild Beast of Prey, now scour abroad, to gorge their craving Maws; the pleasure of Hypocrisie, like a chain'd Lyon, once broke loose, wildly indulges its new Freedom, ranging through all unbounded Joys. (p. 135)

Smuggler recognizes his nephew's voice and is outraged by Vizard's hypocrisy. He considers the young man's monologue to be indecent and profane and decides to foil him. As there is nobody as qualified to unmask a dissembler than another of the same kind, the alderman eventually succeeds in outwitting Vizard. To lead him on Smuggler imitates Lurewell's voice and asks his nephew:

Smuggler.   Where have you left your Sanctity, Mr. Vizard?
Vizard.   Talk no more of that ungrateful subject — I left it where it

	has only business, with Day-light, 'tis needless to wear a Mask in the Dark.
Smuggler.	O the Rogue, the Rogue! — The World takes you for a very sober, virtuous Gentleman.
Vizard.	Ay, Madam, that adds Security to all my Pleasures – with me a Cully-Squire may squander his Estate, and ne'er be thought a spend-thrift – With me a Holy Elder may zealously be drunk, and toast his tuneful Nose in Sack, to make it hold forth clearer. – But what is most my Praise, the formal Rigid she that rails at Vice and men, with me Secures her loosest Pleasures, and her strictest Honour – she who with scornful Mien, and virtuous Pride, disdains the name Whore, with me can Wanton, and laugh at the deluded world. (p. 136)

Both hypocrites are foiled in their plan to seduce Lurewell, and Vizard, who also has to face Smuggler's anger, loses his chance to inherit his uncle's fortune.

Another old and greedy dissimulator is Shadwell's Scrapeall, "a hypocritical, repeating, praying, Psalm-singing, precise fellow, pretending to great piety, a godly knave, who joyns with Cheatly, and supplies young heirs with goods and money" only to gain their confidence and inheritance.[44] Scrapeall pretends to holiness because "it gets him many a good Trust and Executorship",[45] and brings him profitable business. Though he "prays so loud that he is a disturbance to his Neighbours",[46] he is ready to marry his daughter and his niece to those who will pay the highest prices for them. The girls' governess is not much better than Scrapeall. She is an "old Wall-eyed Hypocrite"[47] who forbids the girls to read poetry and only allows books like *A Treatise on Sabbath-breakers,* or, *A Caustick, or Corrosive, for a Sear'd Conscience,*[48] to be kept in the house. Though he governess preaches against fleshly pleasures, she is both "covetous and Amorous".[49] She is easily bribed by the two young men who are in love with the girls. Without any qualms she opens the door for them at night letting them in for a clandestine visit with her charges.

Another such hypocritical pair are alderman Gripe and the marriage-broker, Mrs. Joyner. Gripe is a "seemingly precise, but a covetous, lecherous, old Usurer of the City",[50] who lusts after young girls, and

44   Shadwell, *The Squire of Alsatia,* p. 207.
45   *The Squire of Alsatia,* p. 217.
46   *Ibid.*
47   *The Squire of Alsatia,* p. 250.
48   *The Squire of Alsatia,* p. 249.
49   *The Squire of Alsatia,* p. 253.
50   Wycherly, *Love in a Wood* in *The Complete Plays,* p. 9.

Mrs. Joyner, "a Match-maker, or precise City-Bawd",[51] is ready to cater to his wishes and procure the object of his desires. The encounter and conversation of these two hypocrites is a fantastic ceremony of pretention. They loudly proclaim each other's holiness, though not without suggestive references to their true and less savory natures.

> Gripe. You are a Nursing mother of the saints
> Through you they gather together,
> Through you they fructify and encrease; and through you
> The Child cries from out the Hand-Basket.
> Joyner. Through you the Virgins are marryed and provided
> For as well; through you Reprobates Wife
> Is made a Saint; and through you the Widow is not
> Disconsolate, nor misses her Husband.
>
> . . . .
>
> You are the Pink of a curtious Alderman.
> Gripe. You are the muffler of Secresy.
> Joyner. You are the Head-band of Justice.
> Gripe. Thank you sweet Mrs. Joyner, do you think
> so indeed? you are –
> You are the Bonfire of Devotions.
> Joyner. You are Picklock and Dark-Lanthorn of Policy;
> Gripe. You are the Cup-board of Charity.
> Joyner. You are the Fob of Liberality.
> Gripe. You are the Rivet of sanctify'd Love of Wedlock.
> Joyner. You are the Picklock and Dark-Lanthorn of Policy;
> And in a word, a Conventicle of Virtues.[52]

After the lengthy introduction and praise the main subject is cautiously approached and Gripe expresses his interest in Mrs. Crossbite's little daughter. The pious Mrs. Joyner promises to go early next morning, "it shall be the first thing I'le do after my Prayer",[53] and persuade the girl to become Gripe's paramour.

In all these examples awareness is mixed with ignorance. The hypocrites consciously assume roles and take pride in their performances. They deliberately exploit others, yet they are often unaware that they themselves are recognized for what they are. Congreve further complicates the issue when he creates his would-be hypocrite, Bellmour. The young man, a rather goodnatured and adventurous gallant, decides to play the hypocrite when he finds out that the pious old Fondlewife has a buxom spouse. Knowing that to gain admittance to her he has to disguise himself, he dons the clothes of a puritan preacher. Bellmour ad-

---

[51] *Ibid.*
[52] *Love in a Wood*, p. 14.
[53] *Love in a Wood*, p. 15.

mires himself dressed in the "fanatic habit"[54] and, after asking his friend "does my hypocrisy fit me?"[55] and being assured that it does, he sets out for his adventure.

Though the gallant wears the cloak of sanctity and fancies himself "the very picture of Montufar in *The Hypocrites*",[56] he makes a grave mistake. Bellmour is aware that a puritan preacher should carry a prayer-book, but as he has none handy, he takes with him one of "trusty Scarron's novels",[57] *The Innocent Adultery,* and pretends that it is the holy book. Bellmour the "stalking form of godliness"[58] is unmasked by this mistake. He blames his misfortune on luck: "Damned chance! if I had gone a-whoring with *The Practice of Piety* in my pocket, I had never been discovered."[59] Bellmour's failure is amusing but it is difficult not to sympathize with his plight, whereas the laughter at the expense of real hypocrites is without exception contemptuous.

In Restoration Comedy one encounters only few women who sham holiness, but one can find an endless array of ladies who pretend to be virtuous when they are not. Wycherly's Horner does not feel that one kind of dissimulation is better than another. He addresses a prude with: "You Bigots in Honour, are just like those in Religion; they fear the eye of the World, more than the eye of Heaven, and think there's no virtue, but railing at vice; and no sin, but giving scandal: They rail at a poor, little, kept Player, and keep themselves some young, modest Pulpit Comedian to be privy to their sins in their Closets, not to tell 'em of them in their Chappels."[60] Wycherly's portrait of Mrs. Joyner in his first play *Love in a Wood* is already a pungent criticism of hypocrisy. In *The Country Wife* one encounters the four bigots of honor, the ladies of the Fidget family, and in Wycherly's last and darkest play *The Plain Dealer* one meets the female arch-hypocrite, Olivia.

The reader is already prepared in the "Epistle Dedicatory to my Lady B" for a treatise on hypocrisy. The dedication is addressed to Lady B., Mother Bennet, the well known procuress. First, Wycherly complains that in these evil times no one can distinguish the good women from the evil ones because all are play-acting. "For by that Mask of modesty, which Women wear promiscuously in publick, they

---

[54] Congreve, *The Old Bachelor* in *Complete Plays*, p. 76.
[55] *Ibid.*
[56] *The Old Bachelor*, p. 81.
[57] *Ibid.*
[58] *The Old Bachelor*, p. 95.
[59] *The Old Bachelor*, p. 91.
[60] Wycherly, *The Country Wife*, p. 324.

are all alike, and you can no more know a kept Wench from a Woman of Honour, by her looks than by her Dress." [61] Wycherly ironically praises Mother Bennett's straightforwardness and lack of dissimulation and finally compliments her for remaining true to her profession even in her old age. "Whatsoever your Amorous misfortune have been, none can charge you with that heinous, and worst of Womens Crimes, Hypocrisie; nay, in spight of misfortunes or age, you are the same Woman still." [62]

In the bitter comedy that follows the dedication one encounters Olivia, who was once Manly's love and is now married to his best friend, Vernish. Manly, a sea-captain who returns after a long voyage, still believes that Olivia is faithfully waiting for him and that his friend Vernish is safely keeping his fortune which he entrusted to him. Both are villains and hypocrites whose only aim is to exploit the unsuspecting Manly.

Olivia knows that the misanthropic Manly would be attracted by a woman of the same temperament. She admits in one of her more honest moments: "I knew he lov'd his own singular moroseness so well, as to dote upon any Copy of it; wherefore I feign'd an hatred to the World too, that he might love me in earnest: but, if it had been hard to deceive him, I'm sure 'twere much harder to love him" (p. 482).

Olivia dissimulates not only when she is in Manly's company but also when she is with her cousin Eliza. Eliza quickly perceives the discrepancy between her cousin's statements and actions. When Olivia describes herself she paints the picture of a virtuous woman who abhors flattery, gossip, and who shuns the courtiers and the theatre. Soon Eliza discovers that her cousin thrives on flattery and does not only enjoy hearing others railing but is herself the most vicious gossip. As for the theatre, Olivia describes with great relish scenes from *The Country Wife*, yet complains about "the clandestine obscenity in the very name of Horner" (p. 420). The way she relates the various scenes of the play shows her smutty mind and her love for obscenities.

Olivia.   ... for when you have those filthy creatures in your head once, the next thing you think, is what they do; as their defiling of honest Mens Beds and couches, Rapes upon sleeping and waking Countrey Virgins, under Hedges, and on Haycocks: nay, farther –.

[61]   Wycherly, *The Plain Dealer*, p. 380.
[62]   *The Plain Dealer*, Epistle Dedicatory, p. 383. Further references to this play are given in text, by page-numbers.

Eliza.   Nay, no farther, Cousin, we have enough of your Comment
                on the Play, which will make me more asham'd than the Play
                it self. (p. 421)

Olivia is ready to explain in detail "the filthiest thing in the play" (p.
421) and succeeds in doing so despite Eliza's protests.

After repeated indiscretions Olivia begins to suspect that her actions
are censored by others. Like most of the hypocrites she is very much
concerned with her reputation and wonders if the "world" is talking
about her. Eliza, who is annoyed by her cousin's pretentions and is upset by her ill-natured ways, assures her that the world is indeed talking
of her, saying that she pretends to hate men only so "that the Wives
and Mistresses may not be jealous" (p. 489). Olivia is outraged when
she hears all this but Eliza continues to tell her that others believe,

Eliza.   That you condemn the obscenity of Modern Plays, only you
                may not be censur'd for never missing the most obscene of the
                old ones.
Olivia.   Damn'd World!
Eliza.   That you deface the nudities of Pictures, and little Statues
                only because they are not real.
Olivia.   O fie, fie, fie; hideous, Cousin! The obscenity of their Cen-
                sures makes me blush. (pp. 489-490)

The gullible Manly also discovers that Olivia's "like a Pyrat" deceived him by "spreading false Colours" (p. 431). She and the treach-
erous Vernish robbed him of his money and also of his belief in humanity. It takes the love of Fidelia and the loyal Freeman to convince
him that there are still "Good-natur'd friends, who are not Prostitutes
And handsome Women; worthy to be Friends" (p. 515). Wycherly's
comedy is dark and the villains nearly succeed in destroying their victims.

Restoration playwrights, when they depict the darker side of life,
seem to feel the same way as Molière does, that hypocrisy is a dangerous vice, *"celui-ci est, dans l'Etat, d'une consequence bien plus
dangereuse que tous les autres"*,[63] and also, that dissimulation is often
successful and can play havoc with people's lives. Tartuffe is capable
of outwitting his victims and only the miraculous intervention of the
King saves Orgon and his family from destruction. Many of the hypocrites are clever enough to direct the lives of others and victimize not
only the gulls but also the knowledgeable and virtuous people who are
willing to take them at their face value. The hypocrites are either

[63] Molière, Preface to *Tartuffe* (Paris: Librairie Larousse, 1964), p. 28.

stripped of their pretentions by those who are more clever than they are or, as in Tartuffe's case, their downfall is due to their exaggerated self-esteem and pride in their villainy and showmanship. Vizard, who fancies himself to be a great stage-villain, oversteps the bounds of prudence when he soliloquizes about his vices.

Dante sends the hypocrites into nether hell where the fraudulent are punished. They wear heavy cloaks of lead covered with gold to give the appearance of worth and brilliancy. They walk for all eternity oppressed by the weight of their guilt. In the realm of comedy the hypocrite's punishment is ridicule. Molière, who agrees with Congreve and Shadwell that comedy should teach, feels that a serious treatise is less effective in showing the nature of vice than the scathing ridicule of laughter.

Les plus beaux traits d'une sérieuse morale sont moins puissants, le plus souvent, que ceux de la satire; et rien ne reprend mieux la plupart des hommes que la peinture de leurs défauts. C'est une grande atteinte aux vices que de les exposer a la risée de tout le monde. On souffre aisément des répréhensions; mais on ne souffre point la raillerie. On veut bien être méchant; mais on ne veut point être ridicule.[64]

Though Molière contends that people are prepared to be wicked but dislike appearing ridiculous, he does not punish his Tartuffe with laughter. Until the very end, when the King discovers his crimes, he remains a successful and destructive villain. The hypocrites of the Restoration comedy are, on the other hand, frequently chastised by laughter as their dissimulations are discovered and their true natures are gradually exposed. Gilded pretensions are shown to be false and the discrepancy between exaggerated virtue and petty, underhanded vice is revealed. The incongruous juxtaposition of Gripe's zeal and lust, and Joyner's praying and procuring give rise to amusement. The battle which ensues between their two selves and which ends in victory and revelation of the lower instincts has great comic possibilities. When the fancy, gilded, costume slips and the naked, rather unattractive self is exposed, a dignified recovery is hardly possible.

The comic hypocrites, despite their partial awareness which enables them to manipulate others, seldom gain a vision of the unattractiveness of their nature. They cherish their vices and seem to be oblivious of their ugliness. Like Olivia, they rationalize when their viciousness is exposed and accuse the world, luck, and other people for their mis-

---

[64]   Preface to *Tartuffe*, pp. 28-29.

fortune. Though Shadwell hopes that he can render the "Figure of Vice and Folly" so detestable that people will hate the sin "in their dear selves" the examples presented on the stage leave little hope that this is feasible. If a hypocrite regrets anything then it is only his failure to act convincingly and carry his designs to a successful and profitable conclusion.

V

CONCLUSION

Every literature is at least partially the product of its age. In the last decade of the seventeenth century Dryden begins his commendatory verses to Congreve's *The Double Dealer* with: "Well, the promised hour is come at last; / The present age of wit obscures the past."[1] Dryden continues by praising the King's influence on the culture of his age. According to the poet, Charles the Second "Tamed us to manners, when the stage was rude; / And boisterous English wit with art endued."[2] The King, the court, the fashionable set, and the conditions of the time contributed to the shaping of literature. The values presented are those of a successful ruling clique, the microcosm of the courtly society. Its levity and artificiality is mirrored in the contemporary drama together with the disillusionment of a post-war generation. The civil war, the Dutch wars, outbreaks of the plague, and the London Fire, all left their mark on the thinking and behavior of the people. Though in rare instances disasters bring out the best in man, the majority of humanity is revealed at such instances at its worst. Disillusionment with man results in certain attitudes and values which are all present in Restoration comedy: the importance of being able to laugh at one's misfortunes, the emphasis of being aware and resourceful, the lack of illusion, and great dislike for pretentions.

In a world where awareness, wit, and "tamed manners" are of supreme importance the brunt of ridicule falls upon those who are stupid, imperceptive, and ignorant of the rules of proper behavior. Thus in Restoration comedy one encounters most frequently comic characters who lack intelligence and are ignorant of manners.

In the permissive, fast-living circle where promiscuity is condoned,

---

[1] *Commendatory Verses to my dear Friend Mr. Congreve, on his Comedy called "the Double Dealer"* by John Dryden, in: William Congreve, *Comedies*, ed. Bonamy Dobrée (London: Oxford University Press, 1966; first printing, 1925), p. 114.
[2] *Ibid.*

ignorance of morals, and especially sexual morals, is of negligible portance. In the battle of sexes usually not the villainous seducers and adulterers are ridiculed but the losers who were not clever enough to avoid being deceived or who were frustrated in achieving their goals. From the assembly of cuckolds, foiled women, and successful Don Juans one might conclude that only intelligence and inventiveness are extolled in Restoration comedy.

Although playwrights say that they wish to render immorality and vice ridiculous, they seldom succeed in doing so. Congreve's motto for *The Way of the World* comes from a Horatian satire:

> Audire est operae pretium, procedere recte
> Qui moechis non vultis.[3]

> Metuat, doti deprensa.[4]

Though Fainall and the wicked Mrs. Marwood receive their punishment their plight is only a minor event in the play. Those who become the butts of laughter are not the adulterers but the fools, the witwoulds, and the wanton widows.

Though wit is celebrated there are few plays in which one cannot find a value above mere cleverness. Wisdom and morality appear in many forms, though often the characters who represent virtue, goodness, and kindness do not triumph over the practicers. The theatre audience is accustomed to see virtue and justice win over evil. The audience which views the Restoration comedies is therefore disturbed at times when the good characters are given secondary roles and also when they fail to overcome the less reputable elements.

In the age of awareness knowledge of self and others is highly valued. The Restoration playwright is frequently portraying men who do not know themselves and are therefore ridiculous. The authors consistently exploit the comic possibilities of the discrepancy between what man thinks he is and what he actually is.

Knowledge of others is essential to practicers. Those who are aware of others can draw a sharp and amusing picture of the fools who populate their world. Before Petulant and Witwoud enter, Mirabell and Fainall sketch up a devastating image of their foolish appearance and nature. Sparkish's caricature is drawn with bold strokes by the three wits Horner, Harcourt, and Dorilant. It is puzzling though that the

---

[3] Horatio, Lib. I., Sat. 2.
[4] *Ibid.* (Ye that do not wish well to the proceedings of adulterers, it is worth your while to hear how they are hampered on all sides.)

playwrights do not utilize fully the possibilities of presenting comic characters who are ignorant of others. Shakespeare and Jonson seemed to be aware that men who fail to know their fellow beings are ludicrous, but the Restoration playwrights only use the stock-situations and emphasize other kinds of follies. The comic and tragic possibilities of man's misunderstanding of others will be fully realized in later ages by such writers as Chekhov, Ibsen, and Pirandello.

The attitudes and the spirit of the times define the kind of ignorance which is most frequently ridiculed. Similarly the abundance of artificial characters can be partially explained by the influence of the contemporary French theatre, especially by the plays of Molière. Also, the close-knit, intimate social set encourages the lampooning of particular persons and thus one frequently encounters caricatures of well known personages on the stage. Bayes' portrait is the best known but, as Congreve indicates, many attend the theatre to

> Watch plays with scurrilous intent
> To mark out who by characters are meant.
> And though no perfect likenes they can trace
> Yet each pretends to know the copied face.[5]

In his age Aristophanes openly presented caricatures of contemporary public figures, but Restoration playwrights generally avoid such practices and state that they try to paint the follies of the age and not of specific individuals. Yet, it is with good reason that the wits found pleasure searching for the originals of the characters shown on the stage. It is suggested, and not without justification, that Etherege's Dorimant is a portrait of Lord Rochester and that Hewitt is ridiculed in the figure of Sir Fopling Flutter.

Not only caricatures but also types are often utilized in the comedies. Some are traditional figures and others are created by the conditions of the times. The clever servant, the authoritarian father, and the *miles gloriosus* can be traced back through the ages to classical drama. Besides these universal types, one finds figures who are especially characteristic of Restoration comedy. The frenchified fop, the would-be wit, the ridiculous *précieuse,* and the *belle,* are products of contemporary taste. Humor characters are to be found occasionally in the comedies, especially in Shadwell's plays but, perhaps as a reaction to the puritanical attitudes in the earlier decades of the century, writers avoid portraying morality characters.

---

[5] Congreve, *Comedies*, p. 372.

The artificial characters frequently dominate the plays at the expense of the more lifelike semi-fools. In some of the less successful dramas the partially aware are entirely missing and one encounters only the dunces and the all-knowing practicers who rule and direct their grotesque world. Only writers like Wycherly and Congreve consistently populate their comedies with silly-wise fools.

The dunces of Restoration comedy seldom develop or gain insight. After they are ridiculed, many are forced to realize that they were wrong but no real change in their nature results. One feels that they will commit the same mistake in the future if the opportunity presents itself. The only convincing changes in comic characters happen in the cases of Wycherly's Margery Pinchwife and Congreve's Prue. Usually characters change from worse to better but in these two we have a comic inversion of the accepted norms. Like Pygmalion, they go through a learning process, but instead of gaining awareness they seem to be even more ignorant by the end of their education than they were before. They acquire the knowledge of some rather questionable manners but in doing so, their complete ignorance of morals is revealed.

In the age of awareness the playwright, conscious of all the intricacies of his craft, ponders its nature and possibilities. The Restoration author knows how to create a successful comic character – at least he knows in theory. In the dedications, prologues, and epilogues of various plays one finds numerous passages describing the proper way of depicting fools. The dramatists unanimously condemn those who create crudely drawn and highly exaggerated characters. Dryden is especially adamant in voicing his opinion of contemporary playwrights who follow the wrong practices.

> Most modern wits such monstrous fools have shown,
> They seem'd not heaven's making, but their own.
> Those nauseous harlequins in farce may pass,
> But there goes more to a substantial ass;
> Something of man must be exposed to view,
> That, gallants, they may more resemble you. [6]

Dryden suggests that a comic character should be lifelike. To create a living figure is a difficult task for any playwright because he cannot include all the traits of a personality in a portrait. The author has to be selective and combine only the most outstanding characteristics of his

---

[6]   Sir George Etherege, *The Man of Mode*, Epilogue by Mr. Dryden in *Plays and Poems*, ed. and intro. A. Wilson Verity (London: John C. Nimmo, 1888), p. 373.

personage. If he limits himself only to one trait, his stage-fool easily becomes artificial and mechanical. The Restoration dramatists are aware of this and demand variety. Congreve states:

> For well the learned and judicious know
> That satire scorns to stoop so meanly low,
> As one abstraced fop to show.
> For, as when painters form a matchless face,
> They from each fair one catch some different grace;
> And shining features in one portrait blend,
> To which no single beauty must pretend.
> So poets oft do in one piece expose
> Whole belles-assemblees of coquettes and beaux.[7]

Shadwell in his Prologue to *The Virtuoso* also explains his intent to create diversity in his comedy by showing:

> Such Fools as haunt and trouble Men of Wit,
> And spight of them will for their Pictures sit.
> Yet no one Coxcomb in this Play is shown,
> No one Man's humour makes a part alone,
> But scatter'd follies gather'd into one.[8]

The variety includes not only several traits combined in one person but also several kinds of fools in one play. If one dunce dominates the comedy it easily becomes a farce – for example, Buckingham's *The Rehearsal*. In his Prologue to *Sir Martin Mar-all* Dryden explains how he "hunted" for his characters and then "cooked up" a successful comedy.

> Fools, which each man meets in his Dish each Day
> Are yet the great Regalios of a Play;
> In which to Poets you but just appear,
> To prize that highest which cost them so dear:
> Fops in the Town more easily will pass;
> One story makes a statuable Ass:
> But such in Plays must be much thicker sown,
> Like yolks of Eggs, a dozen beat to one.
> Observing poets all their walks invade,
> As men watch Woodcocks gliding through a Glade:
> And when they have enough for Comedy,
> They stow their several Bodies in a Pye.

---

[7] Congreve, Epilogue to *The Way of the World* in *Comedies*, p. 372.
[8] Thomas Shadwell, Prologue to *The Virtuoso* in *The Complete Works of Thomas Shadwell,* ed. Montague Summers (London: The Fortune Press, 1927), Vol. III, p. 103.

The Poet's but the Cook to fashion it,
For, Gallants, you your selves have found the wit.[9]

The analytical statements of these writers remind one of Socrates' remarks about the poets. In his search for truly wise men he questioned
the greatest poets of his time and discovered that, although they create
great literary works, they cannot explain how and why they wrote
them. Many of the Restoration playwrights are able to explain what
they ought to do but when it comes to creating great works of art they
fall short of perfection.

Though the spirit of the times and even knowledge of literary practices help to shape the drama of the age, in the final analysis the nature of the artistic work and its success depends on the individual
writer. As Dryden aptly remarks when he praises Congreve: "Time,
place, and action may with pains be wrought / But genius must be
born, and never can be taught."[10]

Shadwell and Dryden are occasionally blessed with the gift of the
Muses but their plays and comic characters are frequently artificial
and contrived. Shadwell's fools are usually possessed by one humor
and their rigidity and fantastic ignorance makes them more suitable
for farce than comedy. Occasionally Shadwell succeeds in creating
variety and produces rather delightful plays like *The Squire of Alsatia*,
and *The Sullen Lovers*. Dryden is also erratic in his portrayal of comic
characters. Sometimes his dunces are grossly mechanical as in the case
of Sir Martin Mar-all and other times he creates silly-wise fools who,
like Melantha, are charming and alive.

Etherege depicts with wit and sophistication, but without genius,
the stock-characters of his time. Because he avoids excess and gross-
ness he manages to give an illusion of reality to his wanton wife, foolish
husband, fluttering fop and arrogant courtier. One feels that he is educated and aware of the world around him but that his talent suffices
only to sketch a delightful caricature of an acquaintance or draw a
vignette of a drawing-room scene.

Wycherly's dynamic comedy bears witness to the author's talent.
The comic characters are often both conventional and original at the
same time. Wycherly, greatly influenced by Molière, utilizes types in
his plays, yet he endows them with unusual qualities. The Widow

[9]   John Dryden, Prologue to *Sir Martin Mar-all* in *The Works of John Dryden*,
ed. John Harrington Smith and Dougald MacMillan (Berkeley and Los Angeles:
University of California Press, 1962), Vol. IX, p. 208.
[10]   Commendatory Verses, *Comedies, Congreve*, p. 115.

Blackarce is an atypical widow and Margery Pinchwife, an ignorant country-wife, surprises us by growing into a devious practicer. Wycherly often deals with obsessions and portrays rigid characters but they are never monstrously stupid or mechanical. Even his fools possesss some kind of awareness and he manages to present the kind of variety which gives the necessary scope and complexity to a successful comedy.

Wycherly's latest comedies are dark, not because man is portrayed as being hopelessly ignorant but because his world is populated and ruled by men who are aware but evil. Poetic justice is not possible in the realm ruled by the Horners. The hypocrites and adulterers go free and those who are good remain only shadowy figures in the background. The rogue pulls the strings in Wycherly's comedy whereas Congreve's kingdom is ruled by brilliant and often benevolent forces.

Congreve's characters, and especially his silly-wise fools, have their shortcomings but they are seldom evil. They exist in a sunny realm where beside cleverness other values are also appreciated. Congreve has definite theories about the nature of a comic character and he is able to realize his ideas and put them into practice. He explains that he does not portray gross fools because "they should rather disturb than divert the well-natured and reflecting part of the audience".[11] Therefore Congreve decides to "design some characters which should appear ridiculous, not so much through natural folly (which is incorrigible, and therefore not proper for the stage) as through affected wit".[12]

Thus Congreve's comic characters seldom come from the category of the ignorant. Though his fools are vain and not too intelligent they are frequently blessed with self-awareness and even awareness of other people. In his last two plays Congreve eliminates characters who are altogether ignorant and presents only silly-wise fools and those who are aware.

When Congreve utilizes types he transforms them into very particular individuals. The clever servant is changed into the university-educated and all-knowing Jeremy of *Love for Love* and the tactful and gentlemanly Waitwell of *The Way of the World*. They are the first comic English butlers, individuals, who eventually will become types in the coming centuries.

---

[11] Congreve, *Comedies*, p. 292; Dedication to the Right Honourable Ralph, Earl of Montague by Congreve.
[12] *Ibid.*

Dryden recognizes Congreve's genius and pays tribute to the young writer when *The Double Dealer* is performed.

> In him all the beauties of this age we see,
> Etherege his courtship, Southerne's purity;
> The satire, wit, and strength of manly Wycherly. [13]

A few years later Richard Steele writes his "Commendatory Verses to Mr. Congreve, occasioned by his Comedy called 'The Way of the World' ". He praises the lifelike quality and humanity of Congreve's world. He states:

> By your selected scenes and handsome choice
> Ennobled Comedy exalts her voice;
> You check unjust esteem and fond desire,
> And teach to scorn what else we should admire:
> The just impression taught by you we bear,
> The player acts the world, the world the player. [14]

The master of Restoration comedy is Congreve who creates charming, sympathetic silly-wise fools. The other writers of this period are less successful when they attempt to create the more mechanical characters. But, one has to remember the fools of Aristophanes, Plautus, Boccaccio and Molière to realize that even the most ignorant, contemptuous and artificial dunces can be magnificent and successful comic creations. In most instances, when one deals with the silly-wise fools of Congreve or the ignorant dunces of Boccaccio, the ignorance-awareness chain enables the reader to gain insight into that which is inherently comic in a character. It helps to define the "comic flaw", the particular weakness which often happens to be some kind of unawareness. Such an approach reveals also the complexities of a character and helps discern, as for example in Wycherly's case, ironies which enhance the make-up of a comic figure.

Most theories of literature have their limitations and this is true also for the ignorance-awareness chain developed and then applied to Restoration Comedy. It remains an approach – one way of looking at the infinite variety of the comic. It is an approach by which not only the nature of a comic character can be evaluated but which also helps to illuminate the comic trends of a period, the comic style of a writer, and the make-up of a particular comedy.

---

[13] Commendatory Verses, *Comedies,* Congreve, p. 290.
[14] *Ibid.*

Addison, Joseph, *The Spectator* (London: George Routledge and Sons, 1757).
Addison, Joseph, *The Works of Joseph Addison* (New York: Harper, 1850).
Aristotle, *Nicomachean Ethics*, trans. Martin Ostwald (The Library of Liberal Arts: Bobbs-Merrill, 1962).
—, *The Art of Rhetoric*, trans. John Henry Freese (London: Harvard University Press, 1967 [1926]).
Aristotle's Theory of Poetry and Fine Art, ed. S. H. Butcher (New York: Dover, 1951).
Auden, Wystan, "Notes on the Comic", *The Dyer's Hand* (New York: Random House, 1962).
Baudelaire, Charles, "On the Essence of Laughter", *The Mirror of Art*, trans. Jonathan Mayne (London: Phaidon, 1955).
Bergson, Henri, "Laughter", in *Comedy*, with George Meredith, ed. Wylie Syper (Garden City, N.Y.: Doubleday and Company, Inc. [Anchor Books], 1956).
Berkeley, D. S., "Penitent Rake in Restoration Comedy", *Modern Philology*, XLIX (1952), pp. 223-233.
Blistein, Elmer. M., *Comedy in Action* (Durham, N.C.: Duke University Press, 1964).
Borev, Jurii Borisovich, *Über Das Komische*, trans. from Russian, Plavius von Heinz (Berlin: Aufbau Verlag, 1960).
Bossuet, J. B., *Maximes et Réflexions sur la Comédie*, ed. G. Soury (Paris: Hatier, 1925).
Bronson, B. H., *et al., Studies in the Comic* (Berkeley: University of California Press, 1941).
Buckingham, George Villiers, 2d Duke of, *The Rehearsal*, ed. and intro. Montague Summers (Stratford-Upon-Avon: The Shakespeare Head Press, 1914).
Carlyle, Thomas, *Critical and Miscellaneous Essays* (Chicago: Belford, Clarke, 1880).
Castiglione, Baldasar, *The Book of the Courtier*, trans. and ed. Friench Simpson (New York: Ungar Publishing Company, 1959).
Cazamian, Louis, "Why We Cannot Define Humor", *Revue Germanique*, 1906.
—, *The Development of English Humor* (Durham, N.C.: Duke University Press, 1952).
Cicero, *De Oratore*, trans. E. W. Sutton (London: Harvard University Press, 1967 [1942]).
Clark, Barrett H., *European Theories of the Drama* (New York and London: Appleton and Co., 1918, 1929).
Congreve, William, *Comedies*, ed. Bonamy Dobree (London: Oxford University Press, 1966 [1925]).

—, *Complete Plays*, ed. Alexander Charles Ewald (New York: Hill and Wag, 1964 [1956]).

Cook, Albert, *The Dark Voyage and the Golden Mean* (New York: W. W. Norton, 1966).

Cooper, Lane, *An Aristotelian Theory of Comedy* (New York: Harcourt, 1922).

Corrigan, Robert W., *Comedy, Meaning and Form* (San Francisco: Chandler, 1965).

Critical Essays of the 18th Century, ed. W. Durham (New Haven: Yale University Press, 1915).

Dennis, John, *The Critical Works of John Dennis*, ed. Edward Niles Hooker (Baltimore: Johns Hopkins Press, 1939).

Dobree, Bonamy, *Restoration Comedy* (London: Oxford University Press, 1962).

Dramatic Theory, compiled by Richard B. Vowles (New York Public Library, 1956).

Draper, John W., "Theory of the Comic in Eighteenth Century England", *The Journal of English and Germanic Philology*, XXXVII (1938), 207-223.

Dryden, John, *The Works* (Edinburgh: William Peterson, 1883).

—, *Three Plays*, ed. George Saintsbury (New York: Hill and Wang, 1958).

—, *The Works of John Dryden*, ed. John Harrington Smith and Dougald MacMillan (Berkeley and Los Angeles: University of California Press, 1962).

Eastman, Max, *The Sense of Humor* (New York: Scribner, 1921).

—, *Enjoyment of Laughter* (New York: Simon and Schuster, 1936).

Emerson, Ralph Waldo, "The Comic", *The Complete Works* (Boston: Houghton Mifflin, 1903-1904).

Enck, John J., *Jonson and the Comic Truth* (Madison: University of Wisconsin Press, 1966).

Enck, John J., Elizabeth T. Forter, and Alvin Whitley, *The Comic in Theory and Practice* (New York: Appleton Century Crofts, 1960).

Erasmus, Desiderius, *In Praise of Folly*, trans. John Wilson (Ann Arbor, Michigan: The University of Michigan Press, 1958).

Esar, Evan, *The Humor of Humor, The Art and Techniques of Popular Comedy* (New York: Bramball Howe, 1952).

Etherege, Sir George, *Plays and Poems*, ed. and intro. A. Wilson Verity (London: John C. Nimmo, 1888).

Evans, Bertrand, *Shakespeare's Comedies* (Oxford: Clarendon, 1960).

Farquhar, George, *The Complete Works of George Farquhar* (New York: Gordian Press, 1967 [1930]).

Felheim, Marvin, *Comedy, Plays, Theory and Criticism* (New York: Harcourt Brace, 1962).

Feibleman, James, *In Praise of Comedy* (London: Russel, 1939).

Fielding, Henry, *Joseph Andrews*, ed. Martin C. Battestin (Boston: Houghton Mifflin [Riverside Edition], 1961).

Fitzgerald, P. H., *Principles of Comedy and Dramatic Effect* (London: Tinsley, 1870).

Freud, Sigmund, *Jokes and Their Relation to the Unconscious*, trans. James Strachey (New York: W. W. Norton, 1960).

Fry, William F., *Sweet Madness: A Study of Humor* (Palo Alto, California: Pacific Books, 1963).

Frye, Northrop, *Anatomy of Criticism* (Princeton: Princeton University Press, 1957).

Fujimura, Thomas H., *The Restoration Comedy of Wit* (Princeton, N.J.: Princeton University Press, 1952).

Gilbert, Allan H., *Literary Criticism, Plato to Dryden* (Detroit: Wayne University Press, 1962).

Grant, Mary A., *The Ancient Rhetorical Theories of the Laughable* (= *University of Wisconsin Studies in Language and Literature*, XXI) (Madison, 1924).

Gregory, J. C., *The Nature of Laughter* (London: Paul, 1924).

Greig, J. Y. T., *The Psychology of Laughter and Comedy* (New York: Dodd, Mead and Company, 1923).

Grotjahn, Martin M. D., *Beyond Laughter* (New York: McGraw Hill, 1957).

Hazlitt, William, *Lectures on the English Comic Writers* (New York: Doubleday and Company, 1966 [1819]).

Hamilton, Edith, *The Greek Way* (New York: The New American Library, Mentor Book, 1960 [1948]).

Hegel, G. W., *Philosophy of Fine Art*, trans. F. Osmaston (London: G. Bell and Sons Ltd., 1920).

Herrick, Marvin T., *Comic Theory in the Sixteenth Century* (Urbana: University of Illinois Press, 1964).

Hobbes, Thomas, *Leviathan*, ed. Michael Oakeshott (Oxford: B. Blackwell, 1960).

Holl, Karl, *Aus der Geschichte der Lustspieltheorie* (Berlin: Felber, 1911).

Holland, Norman N., *The First Modern Comedies* (Cambridge: Harvard University Press, 1959).

Hoy, Cyrus. E., *The Hyacinth Room* (New York: Knopf, 1964).

Johnson, Samuel, *Rambler* in *British Essayists*, Vol. XIII (London: Dove, 1827).

Jones, Joseph, "Emerson and Bergson on the Comic", *Comparative Literature, I* (Winter, 1949).

Junger, Friedrich, Georg, *Über das Komische* (Zurich: Verlag Der Arche, 1948).

Kant, Immanuel, *Critique of Judgment*, trans. J. H. Bernard (New York: Hafner Publishing Company, 1951).

Kerr, Walter, *Tragedy and Comedy* (New York: Simon and Schuster, 1967).

Kinderman, Heinz, *Meister der Komödie* (Wien: Donav, 1952).

Koestler, Arthur, *Insight and Outlook* (Lincoln, Nebraska: University of Nebraska Press, 1949).

—, *Act of Creation* (New York: Macmillan Company, 1964).

Krishna, Menon V. K., *The Theory of Laughter* (London: Allen and Unwin, 1931).

Krutch, Joseph Wood, *Comedy and Conscience After the Restoration* (New York: Columbia University Press, 1949).

Lalo, Charles, *Esthétique du Rire* (Paris: Flammarion, 1949).

Lamb, Charles, "On the Artificial Comedy of the Last Century", *The Works in Prose and Verse of Charles Lamb*, ed. Thomas Hutchinson (London: Oxford University Press, 1908).

Langer, Susanne K., *Feeling and Form* (New York: Scribner, 1953).

Latour, Marius, *Le problème du rire et du réel* (Paris: Presses Universitaires de France, 1956).

Lauter, Paul, *Theories of Comedy*, ed. and intro. by Paul Lauter (New York: Doubleday, 1964).

Leacock, Stephen B., *Humor: Its Theory and Technique* (New York: Dodd, Mead and Company, 1935).

—, *Humor and Humanity* (New York: Holt, 1938).

Lessing, Gotthold, *Laocoon* (New York: Noonday Press, 1957).

Ludovici, Anthony M., *The Secret of Laughter* (London: Constable, 1932).

Mahly, Jakob, *Wesen und Geschichte des Lustspiels* (Leipzig: J. J. Weber, 1862).

Mathewson, Louise, *Bergson's Theory of the Comic in the Light of English Comedy* (= *University of Nebraska Studies in Language, Literature, and Criticism,* V) (Lincoln, 1920).

Mauron, Charles, *Psychocritique du genre comique* (Paris: Corti, 1964).

Meredith, George, "An Essay on Comedy", *Comedy* with Henri Bergson, ed. Wylie Sypher (Garden City, N.Y.: Doubleday and Company, Inc. [Anchor Books], 1956).

——, "Prélude", *The Egoist*, ed. Lionel Stevenson (Boston: Houghton Mifflin, 1958).

Michiels, Alfred, *Œvres Complètes de Regnard* (Paris: Adolphe Delahays, 1859).

Molière, *A Collection of Critical Essays*, ed. Jaques Guicharnaud (Englewood Cliffs, N.J.: Prentice Hall, 1964).

Monro, D. H., *Argument of Laughter* (Notre Dame, Indiana: University of Notre Dame Press, 1963).

Morris, Corbyn, *An Essay Towards Fixing the True Standards of Wit, Humor...*, intro. James L. Clifford (Ann Arbor: The University of Michigan Press, 1947).

Nicoll, Allardyce, *An Introduction to Dramatic Theory* (London: Harrap, 1923).

——, *A History of English Drama 1660-1900* (London: Cambridge University Press, 1961 [1923]).

——, *The Theory of Drama* (New York: B. Bloom, 1966).

Nicolson, Harold, *The English Sense of Humour and Other Essays* (London: Constable, 1956).

Oliver, E. J., *Hypocrisy and Humour* (London: Sheed and Ward, 1960).

Olson, Elder, *The Theory of Comedy* (Bloomington, Indiana University Press, 1968).

Pagnol, Marcel, *Notes sur le rire* (Paris: Nagel, 1947).

Palmer, John, *Comedy* (New York: George H. Doran Company, 1914).

Pepys, Samuel, *Samuel Pepys Diary*, ed. Richard LeGallienne (New York: The Modern Library, Random House, 1956).

Perry, Henry Ten Eyck, *Masters of Dramatic Comedy and Their Social Themes* (Cambridge: Harvard University Press, 1939).

——, *The Comic Spirit in Restoration Drama* (New York: Russel and Russel, 1962).

Piddington, Ralph, *The Psychology of Laughter* (New York: Gamut Press Inc., 1963).

Plato, *The Collected Dialogues*, eds. Edith Hamilton and Huntington Cairns (Pantheon, 1966 [1961]).

Potter, Stephen, *Sense of Humor* (New York: Holt, 1954).

Potts, L. J., *Comedy* (New York: Capricorn, 1966).

Priestley, J. B., *The English Comic Characters* (New York: Dutton, 1966).

Rapp, Albert, *The Origins of Wit and Humor* (New York: Dutton, 1951).

Repplier, Agnes, *In Pursuit of Laughter* (Boston: Houghton Mifflin, 1936).

Richter, Johann Paul Friedrich, *Vorschule Der Aesthetik* (Munchen: C. Hanswer, 1963).

Schilling, Bernard N., *Comic Spirit: Boccaccio to Thomas Mann* (Detroit: Wayne University Press, 1965).

Seward, Samuel S., *The Paradox of the Ludicrous* (Stanford, California: Stanford (Stanford, California: Stanford University Press, 1930).

Seyler, Athene, and Stephen Haggard, *The Craft of Comedy* (New York: Theatre Arts Books, 1966).

Shadwell, Thomas, *The Complete Works of Thomas Shadwell*, ed. Montague Summers (London: The Fortune Press, 1927).

Shaw, George Bernard, *Plays and Players* (London: Oxford University Press, 1955 [1952]).

——, *Complete Plays with Prefaces* (New York: Dodd, Mead and Co., 1963).

Smith, Willard, *The Nature of Comedy* (Boston: R. G. Badger, 1930).

Stael, Holstein, and Anne Louise Germaine, *De la littérature*, ed. Paul van Tieghem, 2 vol. (Geneva: Droz, 1959).

Starkie, W. J. M., "An Aristotelian Analysis of 'The Comic' ", *Hermathena* (peri-
    odical), No. 42 (Dublin, 1920), pp. 26-51.
Sully, James, *An Essay on Laughter* (London: Longmans Green, 1907).
Swabey, Marie Collins, *Comic Laughter* (New Haven: Yale University Press, 1961).
Sypher, Wylie, "The Meaning of Comedy", *Comedy* with Henri Bergson and
    George Meredith, ed. Wylie Sypher (Garden City, N.Y.: Doubleday and Com-
    pany [Anchor Books], 1956).
Traherne, Thomas, *Christian Ethics* (Ithaca, N.Y.: Cornell University Press, 1968).
Villiers, George, Duke of Buckingham, *The Rehearsal*; Richard Brinsley Sheridan,
    The Critic; Preface for *The Rehearsal* and *The Critic*, ed. Cedric Gale (Great
    Neck, N.Y.: Barron's Educational Services, Inc., 1960).
Voltaire, *Candide*, trans. John Butt (Baltimore: Penguin Books, 1965 [1947]).
Vos, Nelvin, *The Drama of Comedy: Victim and Victor* (Richmond, Virginia:
    John Knox Press, 1966).
Weinberg, L. Bernard, *History of Literary Criticism in the Italian Renaissance*,
    Vol. I and II (Chicago, 1961).
Welsford, Enid, *The Fool: His Social and Literary History* (New York: Doubleday,
    1961).
Whipple, Edwin Percy, *Literature and Life* (Boston: Osgood, 1871).
Willeford, William, *The Fool and His Scepter* (Northwestern University Press,
    1969).
Wimsatt, W. K., *English Stage Comedy*, ed. and trans. W. K. Wimsatt (New York:
    Columbia University Press, 1955).
Wycherly, William, *The Complete Plays*, ed. and intro. Gerald Weales (Garden
    City, N.Y.: Doubleday, 1966).

INDEX

Works will be found under the author's
name.

Addison, Joseph, 25, 31, 33; *The
Spectator,* No. 249, 18
Aeschylus, 91
Agnes, 11
Arabian Nights, 46
Aristophanes, 137, 142
Aritotle, 22, 26, 29, 32, 35;
Nicomachean Ethics, 12; *Poetics,* 8
Rhetoric, 15
Arnolphe, 11, 13, 64, 89

Babbit, 16
Barrie, Sir James, 28
Behn, Aphra, 37, 84
Bélise, 19
Bergson, Henri, 13, 19, 21, 22, 25, 28,
31, 32, 33, 34, 35
Boccaccio, Giovanni, 15, 23, 25, 31,
142, *The Decameron,* 8, 10, 26, 46
Buckingham, George Villiers, Second
duke of, *The Rehearsal,* 37-45

Calandrino, 9
Caliban, 17
Callot, Jaques, 45
Candide, 30
Carlyle, Thomas, 32
Castelvetro, Lodovico, 8, 9, 10, 22
Cathos, 13
Cazamian, Louis R., 20
Cervantes, Miguel de, 22; *Don
Quixote,* 12, 14, 31, 34, 87
Chaplin, Charles, 31, 69
Charles II., 16, 72, 91, 122, 135
Chaucer, Geoffrey, 32, 46
Chekhov, Anton, 137
Chrysalde, 13
Cicero, 22

Cléante, 12
Congreve, William, 18, 24, 32, 49, 61,
82, 102, 103, 104, 105, 133, 137,
138, 139, 141;
The Double Dealer, 47, 77-78, 80,
92-93, 122, 125, 135;
Love for Love, 66-69, 74, 76, 84,
89, 108-111, 115, 123, 125, 129-
130, 141; *The Old Bachelor,* 65-
66, 80, 84;
The Way of the World, 11, 46, 49,
56-60, 69-71, 74, 78, 79, 84, 90,
136, 141
Cook, Albert, 15
Cunegonde, 30
Cusins, 11
Cyrano de Bergerac, 13, 14

Dante, Alighieri, 133
Davenant, Sir William, 37
Dennis, John, 13
Dogberry, 12, 17
Dryden, John, 18, 19, 21, 37, 65, 83,
116, 122, 135, 138, 140, 142
The Conquest of Granada, 37;
Marriage a la Mode, 48, 115, 116-
117; *Sir Martin Mar-All,* 86-88,
89, 139; *Tyrannic Love,* 37;
Eastman, Max, 31, 33, 82
Eliza Doolittle, 30
Etherege, Sir George, 102, 104, 116,
137, 140; *Love in a Tub,* 49, 61, 125;
The Man of Mode, 61, 81, 84, 105,
116, 120-122, 125; *She Would if she
Could,* 49, 52-53, 84, 89
Euripides, *Bacchae,* 11
Evans, Bertrand, 10, 17
Falstaff, 14, 23, 24, 28, 31
Farquhar, George, *The Beaux's Strate-
gem,* 90; *The Constant Couple,* 115,
126-128; *Love and a Bottle,* 49-50,